IT'S FUN TO TEACH

IT'S FUN
TO TEACH

*A book for folks who wish to help
children in the Church School, but
don't know how to start*

by

VICTOR HOAG

MOREHOUSE-GORHAM CO.
New York
1949

DEDICATION

To the many devoted Church School teachers I have known who labored for their Lord—often with inadequate guidance and poor equipment—but who, like parents, saw it through, and *learned by teaching*.

FOREWORD*

Two great problems in Church teaching are to motivate the teachers and then to equip them. The first is the more difficult. It is not easy to get people to do things with enthusiasm, or well. All employers know that their trouble is to get workers interested in their job—making it their own, not doing as little or as poorly as possible, nor resisting it as though they were slaves.

Fortunately for our work in the Church we can appeal to the highest instincts and touch the deepest springs of action. We can, that is, if we understand the *educational method* of getting people into motion. Clergy show that they lack this understanding when they are heard to say, all too frequently, "I am always *looking* for teachers." Or they remark, "My greatest burden is to *find* teachers. They are always quitting. There never seem enough good ones to fill the classes."

But good teachers are seldom found; they are made. And they are made, not in any standard machine, nor even in a training class, but by all the complicated and subtle ways of inspiration, guidance, simple first duties, reading, and year after year of experience.

Teaching is the foremost task of the clergy. But it is actually a duty shared by every Churchman. We need not only well-informed Christians, but teaching Christians. Ideally, every Churchman is to be a teacher, an official and trusted worker for the planting and blossoming of the Faith. We must manage to get more and more of our people willing and able to "give a reason for the faith," not with the partisan ferocity of high school debaters, but with the word that awakens life. As the

* Or, let's call it *Forward*!

Little Minister's mother said to him before his first sermon, "Jamie, mind ye say a good word for Jesus."

These chapters are to be read by teachers and all who have a glimmering of the possibilities of influencing others. They are to be read by the clergy, whose inner conflicts the writer thinks he understands a little. The clergy's task is the educational awakening of all Churchmen within their cure, and all touching their circle. But these chapters are written especially for those many Church men and women who yearn vaguely to be useful, yet cannot imagine themselves as teachers.

The great weakness of our teaching program is the assumption that we are teaching *facts* about Bible and Church, that if we do not know well all the facts we cannot teach. A better view—though still inadequate—is that we teach people, that *people* is the object of the verb *teach*. But, strictly speaking, we can never teach anybody anything *against his will,* that is, without his glad and willing consent and participation. How to win that good will is the whole trick of teaching. We must maneuver to start people teaching themselves, that is, *learning* by all the devices of exploration, self-expression, and the joy of achievement.

The chief difficulty is that the ordinary Christian has no compelling motive for studying at all. Imitation? But so few of his fellows are studying or even talking intelligently about their religion. Curiosity? That has died down with the passing of childhood, and people keep on postponing the day when they shall "do a little solid reading about religion." There remains the motive of service. Here is a motive seldom touched, but possibly the only one that will ever operate very long, or with any vital force. "For their sakes I sanctify myself," said our Lord.

This book aims at a combination of motivation and method. At the moment, the Church seems overly conscious, even self-

conscious, about the content of her tradition. We act like the
new-rich, awkwardly exhibiting our jewels to the world. We
have insisted on showing the Faith in its crystalized forms of
creed, catechism, and ceremonial—the graduation theses of
Christian students of other years. They in their turn learned by
the process of *living* the Faith, and while doing so, produced
formulas and forms. Why cannot we all enjoy the creative
experiences through which they came? For the Christian tradition is a *culture*, a rich stream which bears us all, together, to
the eternal sea. Often, we have only to help people get into the
stream.

It is assumed that we wish more and more of our people to
have the developing joy of being teachers. You never *know*
until you teach. And you are nearer being a teacher than you
think. When you said, "The rector talked me into taking a
class," you admitted that he made an ideal approach, played
upon your best motives, and gave you a momentary inspiration.
It shows that your priest knew how—at the outset, at least—to
touch the springs of action.

"You know you ought to," the rector had said. "You'll never
appreciate your Church until you teach. It will be lots of fun.
. . . and some hard work. You'll have to figure out most of it
for yourself. But I'll be standing by, with plenty of suggestions."

That is the proposition and plan of this book.

Most of the material appeared originally in *The Living
Church* in the department "Talks with Teachers," but has been
largely re-written to develop the argument of this book: How
do you know you can't teach? Or, You, too, can be a Great
Teacher.

Victor Hoag

Tulsa, Oklahoma
Pre-Lent, 1949

CONTENTS

INSTRUCTIONS FOR TAKING

Dive right in. Read as fast and as intensely as possible, and as far as you can this first sitting. The more you swallow in the first dose, the better chance of its affecting you. But don't say we didn't warn you: This is strong medicine, and it is habit-forming!

I. PRELIMINARY CONSIDERATIONS

1. THE NEED FOR A HOBBY

So you admit you ought to have a hobby! Everybody else has one, these days, and you feel a little queer. There is a widespread acceptance of the belief that everyone should be working at some hobby. On one side this is due to the fact that our working hours are shorter, and therefore our leisure time greater. We must fill out the days somehow. We find people all about us doing the strangest things, and we begin to wonder if there isn't something wrong with us.

But the real urge to have a hobby comes not from imitation of others, but from a deep urge to be doing something yourself, just because you want to do it, and as a continuing interest. Not just a single experience, you feel, but something to be rounded out over the years, to grow old with, like a friend. You have often wondered what would interest you, once you really got started. You don't exactly care to admit that you need such a childish thing as "self-expression," and yet down deep you have a suspicion that it must be something like that. Something within you which has never come to the light. . . . A talent that you have left sleeping too long. . . . It would give you a thrill to do something you have really always wanted to do. . . . To get started. . . . What shall it be?

Yes, you admit, you must get a hobby. You have known it for some time. You may laugh at the queer hobbies of some of your friends, but secretly you envy them. They are definite, happy, busy. There is something respectable about having an interest. If you have come to this state, read these pages warily, but with an open mind. If all goes well, you may be opening a new chapter in your life. This may be it!

There are plenty of people willing to help you choose a hobby and get started. The list of hobbies is, in truth, as long as the list of transitive verbs in the language. There are collections, sports, musical and handicraft specialties. In most of them you will already find plenty of enthusiasts willing to answer your simplest questions, and any number of firms ready to sell you all the equipment. There is a hobby magazine to link the experts into a fraternity, and to interest new recruits. There are bulletins for each of the specialized crafts.

There are five fundamental urges which impel us all to individual activity, differing only slightly in individuals. A few have them all, fully developed and in use. Others are aware of only one or two of these desires. The five urges are (1) to be helpful; (2) to control other people; (3) to do it yourself (which includes making things, sports, artistic expression, invention, exploration, and research); (4) to be recognized (appreciated, admired, or loved); (5) and to possess.

With a little analysis, it will be seen that every one of these applies to teaching in the Church School, in about the order given of importance. There are several requirements for a good hobby and all have their roots in the five primitive urges to action. First, and underlying all, is the point that you must *do it yourself*, not just watch someone else doing it. You must arrange or dust your own specimens, buy and use the tools of your craft yourself, become at least mildly proficient in the terms, the current trends, and the lore of your field.

Second, a good hobby should be in a *specialized area*, in which one may acquire increasing knowledge as time goes on and may have the satisfaction of posing as something of an expert. Highly specialized knowledge on some fine point *within* this chosen field may come later. There are hobbies within hobbies. The point here is that you can't say you have a hobby if you are interested in all hobbies. You must concentrate on one, make it yours. This produces another value in a hobby: companionship with others of like mind. One of your delights will be to share achievements, inventions, and discoveries with your fellow workers. They will understand, and applaud, or even copy you. Hobbies are, also, for this reason, mildly competitive, because you know that your work is known and observed by somebody, and you want to do your best.

Third, and most important of all, a hobby is *voluntary*, done simply because you choose to do it, and solely for the *love* of doing it. This is the meaning of the *amateur* spirit, which, as you will note, has as its root the Latin verb *amo*, I love.

Considering the work of the Church School teacher for a moment, you may note that it fulfils all the requirements of a good hobby, with endless room to grow, to specialize, and to carry on for years. It is the purpose of this book to start many new Churchmen teaching in the parish school as a delightful avocation. To those who have never taught, let it be said emphatically that here is a life-time hobby, rich in rewards, waiting to be embraced. Once you get warmed up and started, nothing can stop you.

Recalling teachers from many parishes, they fall into two groups. There are first those who never caught the spirit of it before they started. These were in most cases drafted into the service abruptly, never really gave themselves wholeheartedly, and therefore lasted only one season. They were doing it as a favor; they rushed in without any preliminary "tips" and warnings, and never did more than mark time. These now feel inadequate; they *have* taught, they say, and know they aren't any good at it. They may have latent just the qualities and motives required, but it will now be hard to revitalize them.

But there is that second company of those who entered upon teaching gladly, who warmed to it gradually, and who stuck at it until it became one of the enthusiasms of their lives. You are invited to consider becoming one of these.

Some hobbies, it will be noted, deal only with *things*—stamps, weaving, rugs, bugs, water-colors, cards, coins. If you find yourself attracted to such, it may be a sign that you are a bit antisocial and that you need just the approach to human life which teaching can give. You need to work all your life with *people* if you are to remain alive and growing. Teaching deals with life; and that means you are part of the process, and it changes you. Once you have taught a class of alert youngsters for a year, you'll never be the same, small person again.

How can one get started? is naturally the next question. The answer is, you may start anywhere, but *you* must take the step. Drop in at a teachers' meeting, uninvited. That alone, will create quite a sensation. One day, spy out the rector's shelf on religious education, and filch a book that seems to appeal. This is in case you are not quite ready to come out in the open. (Note: Don't try to read the book all the way through; that would kill off your urge. Just read here and there, and get the main ideas, and the terms.)

The rector may have a few small books or leaflets which will be just the thing for you, at this stage. Buy one book for your very own, soon. This really commits you, and in after years you will point to it on your shelf as "The first book I ever owned on religious education." (You may never have read it all the way through, but that doesn't matter. It is a collector's item—to you.)

If any special area has appealed to you by now, begin digging into a little of the material on that. This might be visual devices, dramatics, correct school furniture, handwork, hymns, or story-telling. You may even set yourself up as a small expert in one line, such as memory drill, class games, new art work, or finger-games.

Soon you will be ready for your first actual experience of teaching. Keep on reading and preparing, always; but the real thing is teaching. Offer yourself for some simple job, where you can't fail or become discouraged. (Caution: About now the rector may ask you to take full charge of a class. You should refuse until you have had time to feel the ground, become more sure of this new world of teaching. He, poor soul, may have several teachers who have asked to be relieved, and will clutch at any newcomer. Resist him, resolutely, for the good of the cause. You are going into this thing *right*.)

Perhaps you had best visit several classes; maybe you can get to see two on a given Sunday. Take notes. Watch everything, good and bad. If you are observing a good teacher, you will learn a lot. One time, if it can be arranged, ask the teacher you are to visit for the use of her textbook. You will then come to observe with the lesson material already known to you, and you will see the workings of the older teacher's personal adaptation of it.

The next step would be to become definitely assigned to a class as its associate teacher or "teacher number two." Here you will take over certain parts of the period, by agreement with the principal teacher, and get to know the problems and methods without having to take over the burdens of the whole task of teaching. To be thus an assistant teacher for a whole year is no waste of time, for it will produce a confidence and a sharing in the best methods which no amount of study could do, and it will prevent you from making the many wasteful mistakes you might have made had you been thrown into full teaching without any preliminaries.

If you have a speciality such as teaching the singing of new hymns, new handwork projects and materials, or if you are expert in teaching the catechism, or some special area of drill, you may well use this for a season. It would, for example, give much valuable experience if you could be known as "the lady who teaches the Twenty-third Psalm" for a short period in each class, throughout the department. The main thing at the start is to be in touch with the school, its people and its activities, where your knowledge of details may be increasing without being swamped or confused. You might even act as assistant to the secretary, and, in straightening out the school cupboards, come to know the materials. But start somewhere; be around and near. Read what appeals to you, or is recommended. All this takes time, but is necessary at the start.

Now comes the collector stage, when you start your library, notebooks, and clippings. You will experiment with new kinds of handwork, and correspond with teachers in other parishes. One summer you will go to a Church institute for a week or more and receive intensive inspiration to take back to your parish.

Now you are on the inside, and anything can happen! But, if you have gone thus far, you are one of those who have started a new chapter in your life. You have a hobby! You are one of a goodly fellowship.

2. THE SATISFACTIONS OF TEACHING

A rector, trying to enlist a new teacher, was going through all the usual arguments. Finally the woman said, "It isn't so much my lack of knowledge of the Bible, nor not wanting to give the time. But, frankly, it simply isn't my line. It just doesn't appeal to me!"

There you have the real reason why many of our best Church folk have never taught in the parish school. They simply don't want to, and the Church has not found a way to interest and motivate them. Ideally, the very best Christians should do the teaching, in order that the rising generation may have the best of our tradition. But, in practice, many of our best-informed Churchmen never help with teaching. To make such people *want* to teach, to get them started on this most rewarding of tasks, is the main purpose of this book. If they only realized the need! If they only realized how much they have to offer! If they only knew *what fun it is to teach religion!*

Every human activity has its rewards. The chief of these is the universal sense of pleasure, and even amazement, at one's own achievement. At the end of the day you realize that the glow in your mind comes from the thought, "I did it! I wasn't sure I could, when I started. I never really thought I'd see it through. But I've finished it!" You have tasted the experience of latent power brought into use and the confidence that your urges and abilities can produce results. It is a steadying and uplifting experience to discover that you are not just a dreamer, but that your plans actually carry through. You face the future knowing that you can do it, and similar things, again. This is that *experience of success* without which we would all timidly retire within ourselves and become chronic failures.

This is the first of the rewards of teaching. You bring your best powers to a task and find that you can accomplish amazing things. You need not wonder at others. You can do it yourself. And the qualities called out in teaching are as numerous and as varied as human lives. There is the call for leadership, and with it the planning and preparation by study. You will practice directly all the virtues of patience and charity, loyalty and sincerity. There will be some self-sacrifice, self-control, and self-discipline. In short, you will be increasingly at your best as you continue to teach. You will grow. In teaching, you are acting as the foster-parent of the rising generation, leading them into life.

You will find a *purpose for your religion* at last, when you begin to teach. Sometimes, too late in life, people may find out that they have been developing their own souls by the actions of religion, but have nothing to show for it in lives changed about them. Teaching gives a motive, the highest motive, for all acts of religion, and for all pursuit of knowledge. The reason most Churchmen postpone indefinitely a study of the Faith is that they have no immediate use for further knowledge. Some day, they tell themselves, they intend to ask the meaning of this or that part of the service, or to borrow a book about it. But in teaching, knowledge is called for daily, and you have the necessity to study for a purpose. "For their sakes. . . ."

Intimate *contact with youth* is another special privilege of teachers. Boys and girls live in a world of their own, pushed aside by parents and relatives who are usually too busy to do much more for them than the required policing of the day. Contrary to general thought, many parents spend little time *with* their children, directly entering into their lives. The teacher, in public school and at church, is almost the only close personal adult friend of most children. If you doubt this, consider for a moment some child you know, and try to count how many adults regularly take time to drop their own affairs and enter into his life. There will be the parents, of course, yet few parents regularly take time out, or allow a daily period, to play with their children. There is the favorite aunt, or the uncle who takes the boy fishing, or "has them over to the house" for a special treat. There are those adults who, professionally, or by special inclination or enlistment, give themselves to youth—Cub and Scout and other club leaders, and the few rare persons who undertake to work with children on their own. This is almost the end of the list. There remain only the teachers, paid or volunteer. Unconsciously we have allowed them to bear the whole burden of education, and we turn over our children to them, blindly hoping that all will be well. It means that the teacher, at the moment, has a grave responsibility as well as opportunity.

The teacher will, then, be knowing children as they are, and for their own good. He will work with them, talk and plan, and think their thoughts. He will, that is, if he is a *teacher*, not a lecturer dealing out formal words from the detached rostrum of adult life. And they will enter into his life. He will breathe a less stuffy atmosphere; he will know the fresh, raw urges of growing boys and girls, each running true to his or her own character, as well as to the general type of his age-group. "Teaching keeps you young and alive," any older teacher will tell you. Your pupils will be your friends, now and in the years to come. "A former pupil of mine" is a term of high affection and pride. It is a relation that often brings unexpected joys. In after years, you may be rewarded for the long Sundays of faithful teaching by some call that will mean you have touched a groping life.

I have an old-fashioned book, written in the early years of the Sunday School movement, intended to quicken the devotion and piety of the teacher. The chapter dealing with the "Rewards of Teaching" ends with a parable or promise. The good teacher (we are assured) will, at death, go at once to his reward, to mingle with the angels and citizens of heaven. There he will encounter among the throngs, ever and anon, an individual who will have both face and behaviour strangely *like himself*. Again and again the good teacher meets these marked individuals, with their familiar caste, and finally enquires who they are. "They were your Sunday School pupils on earth," explains an angel. "They bear your stamp forever."

The satisfactions, however, are not only remote, but immediate. The most immediate is the discovery of a genuine vocation and a worthy purpose for your life. It is not only the parish authorities who call you and authorize you to take a class. It is the Great Teacher of all, who puts at the head of all His instructions, "Feed My sheep!"

3. EVERY CHRISTIAN A TEACHER

Throughout the Church, much has been made of the Great Commission of our Lord. It has been repeatedly pointed out that this places upon *every* Christian—not merely the specially selected, trained, and sent—the obligation of being a missionary. We are either to go ourselves, or to help send others, that all the world may be Baptized. So much has this missionary imperative been preached that it has become a by-word, "Every Christian, by virtue of his profession, is a missionary."

The Mormon religion has actually placed this as a requirement of membership, and we hear that any Mormon may be called by his church to give two years of his life to personal missionary adventure, anywhere in the world, at his own expense. The purpose might seem to be that of making more Mormons everywhere, but this is only a lesser outcome of the custom. The real gain (apart from obedience and Church discipline) is that the missionaries must master the facts, ideology, claims, and arguments for their religion, and use them in meeting actual people. This venture, far from being only missionary, is found to be really an educational policy and project. Each returned missionary is fairly certain of being a convinced and loyal Mormon all his life.

Now, if we will only re-read the closing words of St. Matthew's Gospel, we will find that Jesus said, "Go. . . . *teach* all nations, baptizing them. . . . *Teaching* them to observe all things whatsoever I have commanded you: and lo, I am with you always, even unto the end of the world." It takes only ordinary reading to reveal that the baptizing is the result of the teaching. And who can miss the awful conclusion that, *if we do not teach, He will not be with us!*

This is the gospel of the teaching Church. It is actually the "curriculum of experience" laid out for the new Christian from the moment he has matriculated by baptism. He finds himself not only a learner, but a responsible spokesman for the Faith, one who at any time may be called upon to bear witness. In short, he is one of a fellowship of teachers, all alert, laboring to find new pupils and to lead new brethren into the full joy of the Faith. Not words, not formulas, but skilful contacts. In brief—if I make myself clear—the teaching duty inherent in the office of being a disciple is to be fulfilled by personal efforts as a teacher. Each of us is to teach whenever and wherever we have an opportunity, partly to win others, but partly to deepen our own knowledge. Is it too strong to say, not merely that we learn a lot when we teach, but that we *never learn* until we can and do teach?

The person who has not unbent himself to win others is, in the exact phrase of the street, a "big stiff." It changes you. You don't know what you are missing if you have never tried to teach somebody. It is not only the fun and human satisfaction of achievement, but the immediate wonder of seeing the Christian life grow, under your guidance. And, in turn, you find the roots of your own spiritual life reaching out.

We ask our pupils to "give it back." But there is a stage in teaching much higher than that. We ask them to give it back in a form adapted to some particular person. We say, "State this doctrine in a way that would be understood by an eight-year-old child." "Go see Mr.———, a Confirmation prospect, and convince him of the importance of orderly, liturgical worship. Don't argue. Win him. You'll have to do some special studying to prepare for your first call, of course." Just so, every teacher comes to his class preparation with the obligation, "I must make this story real to my Junior High boys—not just any boys, but my class."

If every Christian thus accepts his place as a teacher, whenever an opportunity, formal or accidental, arises, he will be increasingly alert to study the ways and needs of people. If he deals with children, he will study child psychology for the special age he teaches. He will notice the reactions, feelings, prejudices, enthusiasms, and other mental and emotional equipment of each person he is trying to influence. With such a sense of calling, a person will also see in everyone he meets a potential pupil to be stirred and started on the Way.

This realization changes everything. Once you begin to see this primary nerve of the Gospel, you will find it at every turn. Church canvassers must win (that is, educate) the people on whom they call, to pledge their money for the support of the Church's whole work with understanding and zeal. Heads of guilds and circles will provide ingenious and appropriate ways of teaching their members about the Church. Vestrymen aware of the teaching duty will tactfully inject inspirational topics and projects into the meetings of the Vestry. Ordinary folks will begin to see all about them individuals they can help.

As individual Christians awaken to this approach, everything about the parish will grow more educational. You will study cases, plan projects, make yearly programs that increased learning and growth may take place throughout the parish. And all the time, you will be making the most of your opportunities to teach through the systematic work of the Church School. You will do your work there, in whatever capacity you have been accepted, because you believe that you must be a teacher because you are a Christian. You can't escape it, once you see this, and you won't want to. You have made teaching your hobby—yes, your special enthusiasm. But it is, deeper than that, your life's call, as a Christian.

4. THE TEACHER AS FRIEND

We all have memories of our childhood. Among the richest of these are memories of some beloved teacher whose friendship continued long after the class year. In nearly every parish there are one or two veteran teachers who know all the older children in the Church School because they have been through their class. And the children keep them as their friends ever after.

A youth finds himself in trouble. In his distress he phones the one strong, sure friend he can think of, his former Church School teacher—not just any teacher, but the one who became his friend, his own true friend, through the Church. Just to have had such a call made on you is rewarding, a certificate and proof of your success.

What is it that causes some teachers to be soon forgotten, to pass into memory as vague non-entities, while the few are remembered? The difference is hard to discover, but it must have something to do with personal interest, the kindling of that relationship which is best defined as friendship. It is partly a born or achieved characteristic in the teacher, partly a separate accomplishment with each new friend. In part it is an incalculable miracle in the realm of the spiritual. But friendship also has its outward and visible rites which may be learned and observed by any one eager for the inward and spiritual reality.

A story is going 'round the Church of a questionnaire asked some pupils, in order to determine just what they liked most about their favorite teachers, what they disliked. To the latter, one reply was, "We don't like a teacher who is a sourpuss." Let's remember that and put down as our first rule: the teacher shall smile often, and *at individuals*. The small child reports at home, "My teacher likes me. She smiles at me."

But the friendly teacher has more than the bright smile, or even the brilliant, vivacious attention to all and each. He sees his pupils as individuals, each from a different kind of home, each with his own special emotional set-up, attitudes, and pattern of response. Each is a problem to be solved as a teacher; but before that, a person to be known and won as a friend. Therefore, the general attitude must be kindliness, cheerfulness, as of one enjoying the time together. One great trouble with the strict teacher, who secures order by external devices of discipline, is that when these have to be pushed under strain, and when the class's energies get out of hand, there is nothing to employ but more strictness. The kindly teacher, however, having always the good will of his pupils, has but to use a look, a word showing he is displeased by the outburst, and lo, they are quiet again for his sake. They might not so express it, but that is the truth.

No teacher can develop inner antagonisms toward any of his pupils if he is to make them his friends. Some teachers, through their own inadequacy (really a haunting fear, arising from past failures in discipline), look upon certain aggressive children as adversaries. "I'll make that boy behave. He's mean, but watch me—he won't get away with anything with me!" Such an initial attitude, even though later dispelled in actual relations through weeks of class fellowship, is an undercurrent preventing the formation of real friendship. Even though there is nothing said, the children sense it. If you detect this in your own heart, blot it out as quickly as you can. Say, "He's got good stuff in him. He's no sissy. I'm going to make him like me. He'll make a fine friend. And I think he needs me. I must reach him, somehow."

But the attitude of approval, or genial interest in all, changes everything, and most of all the teacher. Feeling he is the friend, willing and accepted, he is more confident, more poised. He is not the slave-driver of a company of crafty savages, who may at any moment take advantage of him. He is among friends, dear friends, and life is good.

"I have friends of all ages," boasted a prominent man. That was a statement of his native human interest, his outgoing self. He liked people for themselves.

For any so inclined, who are eager and willing to make friends, it must be admitted that children are often more rewarding than adults. Consider many of your adult intimates: they have a certain maturity and some experience, and they talk of adult doings, but truly few of them have any vital interests, accurate knowledge, or real charm. They are frankly rather obvious, dull, and tiresome. In contrast, a young friend offers eager interest, fresh enthusiasms, a humbling dependence on your opinions. He needs you, and you know you can help him. Young folks are far more fun, more amusing and stimulating, better company than hundreds of stuffy adults.

The techniques? There are no established ones. My list is not yours. Moreover, conscious straining after popularity stems from a wrong motive and usually misses fire. You cannot buy friendships. Yet in "all sorts of little things that he does for the children" is part of the secret of the beloved teacher's influence. Little gifts, reminders, and rewards help to build up this personal relation, but it is always the motive, the genuine human interest of the teacher, which makes the lasting impression. You had better just make up your mind that you are going to be the friend to all your pupils, and then you will find ways of accomplishing this. A good craftsman, committed to his project, finds his own materials, sharpens, and often invents and makes, his own tools.

It doesn't do much good for teachers to be told, at some meeting, "You should always phone to absentees." The ones interested in every child will have been doing that every week;

the others will not do it anyway. (The beloved teacher has few absentees!)

Clearly, you must know your pupils outside of the class time. Two ways are commonly practiced by the friendly teacher: calling at the homes, to know the child in his setting, to enlist the help of the parents; and arranging parties, excursions, treats now and then. One great teacher made a point of having all the children in his class for dinner at his home, two or three at a time, some time during the year.

In between are the little talks, the special notes, gifts, suggestions, birthdays. These are the things which build friendships which last across the years. Let us repeat: children have few adult friends. They greatly need such steadying and uplifting personal contacts. So the teacher is given his list for the year. "Make them your friends," says the wise pastor, "and you will be able to teach them anything."

5. WHAT DO YOU OFFER?

Frankly, when you face your little class on Sunday morning, what do you have to offer them? Is there any substance, weight, value or worth to the personality behind your lesson? Some of the parents of your pupils may have you catalogued as "a nice young man who has a good influence," or "a devoted Churchwoman who certainly knows all about the Church." Perhaps you have been described in some homes as "not very interesting," or "he lets us do anything."

The important thing is that you bring *yourself* to your teaching—all that you are, from all the years of your whole life. The immediate impact, it is true, comes from your recent preparation, plans, enthusiasms, and aims. But your whole life speaks through. Some people have a hundred vital human qualities to offer; some, only one or two. More will have only a mass of rather vague and colorless life experiences to bring. But whatever you are and have, you can make better use of your equipment.

The teacher who is a little discouraged at his results with his class will be all too ready to admit, "I suppose it's my fault. If I knew more, if I worked harder at my lesson preparation, if I put more force and time and thought and loyalty into it, I know the results would be better." But before you bewail your sins in general, take an inventory to see just what list of your equipment you can draw up.

Temperament. Ask yourself if you have the tone or quality of personality required of a teacher. Are you calm, poised, dignified, steady, purposeful; or are you easily flustered, nervous, resentful and petty? Are you outgoing, interested in people; or retiring, timid and stiff? Well, then, face the great human truth: you can change! That is, you can if you will, and if you keep on willing long enough to work through to solutions. This is a moral problem, the problem of your being a real and effective person, or of admitting that you are a failure. You can change, and you can begin this instant. You can start affirming anew your strong points. You can start overcoming your weak points by doing the opposite.

Maturity. Being young has the disadvantage of lacking a mass of experience, and the weight of accumulated knowledge and certainty. But youth has attack, and ideals, and fresh enthusiasm, and nervous force and endurance. You can't change your age today, but you can be at your best more often than you are. And you can act like an adult, although you may still have many of your childhood impulses and reactions. You can make yourself accept responsibility, and see things through. It is childish to quit, to lose interest, to fluctuate in one's attention and emotional drive.

Knowledge. All that you have ever learned, in school or out, is with you as you teach. You never know when something may be called for. You are not to show off your knowledge, or bring up the remnants of a liberal education as a substitute for a prepared lesson. But you can reënforce a lesson at surprising points by material from your mind. The more you know, the more you have to offer—at the moment, in the emergency. Frankly, do you know anything—much? Teaching gives a fresh motive to study. Have you any background books on the Bible, the Church, or theology? Are you a self-developing, interested, eager person, or just one who lives by the funny papers and the "digest" magazines, and is fast settling down into a middle-aged ignoramus?

Teaching skill. All your teaching is cumulative. You do it better every year. But you can improve your methods by a little study in books, by comparing notes with others, by intensifying your lesson preparation. You can recognize that you are in a rut, and climb out.

Your religion. This is the heart of what you have to offer. All the rest is but the frame for this, the outward form of the sacrament of teaching, bearing the inward and spiritual gift for which alone it is established. You can work at the externals of your religion—your faithful routine of unfailing communions, attendance at services and meetings. You can also work at the inner things—your prayers, your intercessions, your meditations. As you think of your pupils, you will find a fresh motive for approaching God, and a fresh resolution will arise to do better next Sunday. "For their sakes. . . ." you keep thinking.

Then, gathering up all yourself—all your resources of all your past years—you find that you really have something to offer. You have enough. You have the stuff for making a great teacher. In that mind, you will go to class, humbly but confidently.

6. IMPROVING YOUR MOTIVES

The reason some people teach well is that they put their full force of character into the job. They want to do it well. There is, indeed, the success that comes from years of experience, and with it, the satisfaction of getting results. But the great trouble with most teachers is that they are half-hearted.

Who is to blame? Are some folks just that way, anyhow, while others are by nature filled with zeal and the fine force of attack? Possibly, in part, but let's look at a typical case— perhaps yourself.

The rector came to you last fall with this appeal: "Our fifth grade boys need a teacher. Mr. B, who has had them for several years, is moving away. There has never been any substitute teacher. I have gone over my lists again and again, and I feel that you are just the one who can tackle this group. Will you do it?"

You made the usual objections: you didn't know anything about the Bible; you never had taught; you had never been to a teachers' training class. The rector answered all these by saying that he would help you get started, that you would learn as you went along.

Finally, you fell back on the suggestion that he might find others. You said, "Why don't you call on the parents of some of those children? It is their responsibility, first." But finally when the rector had patiently explained that parents, too, have duties, and babies to care for, and that some of them have no personality, education, or ability for teaching, you finally agreed to "help him out for a while."

Thus, reluctantly, you took the text book, and (as the rector had suggested) looked it over and tried to get acquainted with the materials. He promised personal conferences at regular intervals, but he was so busy that it turned out that after one such meeting you were left to carry on alone.

You tackled the class with what equipment you could muster—your dim recollections of your own Sunday School days, colored by the long-cherished thought that, if ever you had it to do, you would make it more interesting. You liked the first few sessions, and looked forward to better discipline and results as weeks went along. But things didn't go smoothly. The pattern of your first failures was repeated. You didn't know how to quell energy, or hold pupils to the topic, or prevent destruction of property. You stopped spending so much time preparing your lesson and tried to do things that would merely interest the children, keep the period from being a riot, and avoid notice by the other classes.

But you stuck, and the weeks dragged along. Now, you look forward to Sunday with little enthusiasm, consider each class period an experience to be lived through, somehow. You have become one of the half-hearted. If you stick through this year, and if you receive some helpful guidance, you may reach the end of your second year with enough experience earned in the field to carry on, and to become a regular and eventually even a joyful and skilful teacher.

If you had been started as a substitute, or in a training class, or at least with some preliminary reading and stimulation of advance enthusiasm, you might have been saved from this wasteful first year of trial and error.

But, granted all too readily that it was the fault of the parish authorities who started you wrongly, you can still make something of your teaching task by your own sincere efforts.

As in all of life, you can improve your motives. The force and ideal resolution of your approach to your task can be increased. Why are you teaching? Why do you stick to it at all? Down deep, you know it is not to please the rector, nor to make a showing to certain people, nor to have a sense of authority over youthful lives. In your best heart, you know it is because you are doing God's work, for His children, and that you have made it your Christian job.

That ideal, dim and seldom faced, needs to be brought up into the light of your daily realization. Talk yourself into a better approach: "I'm a teacher . . . I'm in for it, anyway . . . somebody has to do the tough work. . . . But it's not as bad as it used to be. . . . There are some wonderful boys in the class, perfectly normal. . . . They deserve a better break. . . . Of course, they don't always help me, but they are my problem . . . I must solve them . . . I can—after all, other teachers have."

About now you are facing the weak spots which you have known all along. "I'm going to have a perfect class next Sunday. I'll call up the irregular ones. I'll put over this lesson . . . I'll show them!" Now you are all set. But there remains the deeper kindling, the spark that is required to touch off all this tankful of native fuel.

You are going to say your prayers, offer up your lesson to God, and make this new start your special intention at Communion on Sunday. Then you will be, at long last, out on the broad highway of the Teaching Church, a fellow with that innumerable company of the faithful who have preserved the Faith by the difficult art of teaching. Who knows but what now, someday, you may be acclaimed as one of the great teachers!

7. ACCEPTING YOUR CALL

So your rector has asked you to teach this year. Congratulations! You have been considered worthy to be tried out as a member of a picked group at the heart of the Church's life. You are to be one of those "inside" officials who will shape the rank and file, and also the coming leaders, of the active Church in this generation. About one in every thirty adult members of all the non-Roman Christian bodies in this land share this honor in any given year. But since there are many former Church teachers now inactive—perhaps four for each one now in charge of a class—then about one of every six or seven adults has, at some time, been engaged in parish teaching.

Why some of them quit would be an interesting study. Personal duties and family problems would account for a number. Many are too old. All too many did not make a success of it, and dropped out. Others, no doubt, found that teaching called for more energy than their little store of zeal and patience could supply, and they quit, often at times most distressing to the school and its leaders. Perhaps the greatest loss has come from the number who started out with meager training, and little inspiration, and were left to work through the textbook on their own. No wonder the turnover among Church School teachers is so high.

But you are going to be different. You are going to make this the one great advance step in your grown-up life. You are not just going to "try it out for a while," but you are going to be, henceforth, with increasing effectiveness, in one capacity or another, a Christian teacher. You are—if you are the sort of Churchman your rector believes you to be.

It is easy to imagine how you feel. At first you felt complimented. You are still a little scared. You think of some splendid teachers you have known, and the Sunday School of your youth. You wonder if you can fill the job with your small equipment. You told the rector that you didn't know anything about the Bible, but he brushed that aside. He said he counted on you to keep on studying, and it was time you did, anyhow. Even now you may be regretting that you have signed away all your Sundays.

Look at it, however, from the rector's side. This class needed a teacher. The rector knew enough of your intelligence, personality, and spirituality to believe you might start, and improve. It was a rare compliment. The priest has his school. Much as he might often wish that he might teach them all personally, in small groups or all together, he knows that this is impossible. He has to find teachers, not from some approved and tested list at hand, but from among his own parishioners.

He has his own qualifications, naturally. But, in a given parish, only a few can ever be found to measure up to high standards. Most teachers are in process of being made into fine teachers; they are mid-course. So, if he is an old hand, he will have come to three qualifications for his teachers, in this order of importance: (1) loyalty and zeal; (2) availability; (3) knowledge, skill, and experience. The last can be acquired. If you can meet the first two requirements, you can, on the job, catch up on the third.

Now there are certain things at the start of each year which you, as a teacher, have a right to expect—yes, demand. These are as follows:

(1) You can expect your priest to give you a course or outline for you to follow. You must have both a year's topic or area and a text book. You will find other books to help, and you will add other interesting subjects as you go along, but this back-bone must come from the parish authority. In spite of the truism that "you are teaching children, not lessons," the fact remains that you are teaching the Christian religion, which is no shapeless mass of sentiment, but a substantial body of facts, usages, and disciplines. These have been organized into portions suited to the age of the pupils, and such plans come to us as printed lesson series. It is your priest's duty to select one of these and equip you with it.

(2) You have a right to expect that your priest, or someone

appointed by him, shall have a private session with you to go over your material, before the opening date and about once every month.

(3) You should have correct lists, well in advance. You have a right to a separate room for your class and enough proper equipment with which to work.

And now you are in for it—not just one year of teaching, for teachers, like parents, once in, never quit; they can't. The burden of the growing lives of boys and girls is upon their hearts. Teaching *gets* you. The act of teaching changes the teacher. It demands that you call upon talents hitherto unused and forces never before released. You are not only going to learn as you teach, but you are going to grow in grace.

When you become a teacher, you cease to be a child. Gone must be childish nonsense, flights, evasion, self-indulgence, and pretense. You have become a responsible Christian adult. You will never be the same again. Accept your call then, gladly, seriously. It is from God, through the lips of His minister. As you teach, more may happen to you than to your pupils. Steady then! you are entering a long career. Come well prepared on the opening Sunday to meet your spiritual children.

8. WILL YOU BE READY?

How can we help you, teachers new or old, to make a fine start with your Church School teaching this year? How can we do it, with the limitations of the printed word? Let's see— we might tell you some things to do, and hope that you will read and follow some of our ideas. Here is the list of suggestions:

Get your textbook, and one set of the pupil's materials. Clean up or arrange the corner of your desk at home where you keep your Church School materials. Does it have a Bible, a concordance, modern versions of the Bible, a Hymnal and a Prayer Book? Is your notebook ready, with section headings all made, and all past useless material thrown away? Start a file now for clippings—verse, cartoons, illustrations, games—for ready use. Start a page of projects—possible handwork or activity schemes which might fit your class and the year's theme. Make your class calendar of the main goals, of the special events and feasts, of weekday events, parties, and trips. (You will change this as you go along, but it is something to work toward.) Make a separate list of the memory items you will accomplish during the school year. List all the materials you will need.

A lot of fine things to do, you will admit. More could be thought of. A few teachers might do all of these things, just from reading the above paragraph. Such people are the obedient, the self-disciplined—also they are those who are a little ponderous and methodical. But you would not be apt to do these things just because you saw them in print. Most readers of the above will probably do nothing. These little obvious suggestions from experience will probably soon evaporate, and leave little impression or impulse. You simply will not do them. And I will have failed, as your teacher.

Let me show you a more practical way. And, as I operate, I will show my hand. Let me try to get you to do the above things, but in the educational way. The following is a better approach to you, my problem readers. (Kindly imagine, as you read, that we are in a teachers' meeting, enjoying the inspiration of fellowship, and discussion on each point.)

I must *motivate* you! I must *make you want* to make a perfect start. If I can do that, the details do not matter. I will not have to make many suggestions, and you will yourself invent better ways, or grasp at methods reported, making them your own.

Very well then . . . fresh start. (Slight pause, to catch every eye.) I am asking you to use your memory—think back—recall the very best Church School class you have ever seen. Perhaps it was one in which you were a pupil, under some skilled teacher. Or maybe one you visited. Now, would you like your class to be as fine as that, every Sunday morning, next year? (Discussion here of an ideal class, and some of its ingredients.)

Now, teachers, think of some of those good days when your own class had a perfect lesson. Would you like to repeat those times—the joys of happy fellowship, the after-glow of success felt? Of course you would! (Point of contact with pupil's vital hope-life, his ambitions, fears, emotions, and memories.)

Next I want to ask you, do you really care for children? (Challenge.) Have you shown it in the past, by the way you sometimes failed to prepare your lesson? Just what *are* your motives, down deep: display? a sense of power over young lives? or a spiritual vocation to the ministry of teaching in Christ's name and power?

Let's look at your real job, then. Here is the list of your children for next year. They are your portion of the flock. You know most of them already: Helen, Ruthann, Shirley, and the others. Before you meet them, what are some of the things you might do to prepare? (Notice, I'm not telling you, I'm asking you, working for your response. The leader—that's me—allows one member of class to take chalk and write on the board suggestions offered by the others. The following list might arise from a typical group of teachers.)

Things to Do Before School Opens

Get in contact with parents of my children, by phone, note, or call. Look up in a child-study book the psychological characteristics of this age child. Get sample of all my texts, leaflets, cut-outs. Plan a permanent place in my home for study, keeping all my books and materials there. Decide on the opening project for the first five or six Sundays—a trip to an institution, an All Saints' Day litany, a pilgrimage to the font, or whatever.

Hold that thought of the finest possible class! The best *year* ever! What else do you feel you should do? (I don't want to *tell* you. I want you to say it.) "I think I shall read through the first four or five lessons, to get the feel of my new textbook. And, of course, the introductory pages," somebody proposes. Fine. Now you are in motion. But let's be definite: when? "This week, tonight!"

What about your spiritual attitude this year? Are you going to lead your pupils religiously, in Christ's name, and to Him? Or are you just going to teach Bible stories, Church lore, and induce some activities? What should be *behind* all this busyness? You respond, "I'm sure I ought to read some spiritual book. I'll ask the rector."

And so, at long last, you are being motivated. If you have vibrated to the foregoing at all, you will see what we are after. You knew it all the time! It is not enough to "take the third grade girls next fall." You are going to *give your life*—or at least certain keen hours of it, through many weeks—in loving leadership of these children. Lessons, materials, and activities are the machinery of your work, the frame of your picture. But you are actually teaching *children*, these particular children. They are very precious to their parents—and to God. Look up Malachi 3:17. No, we'll copy it here, to make sure: "And they shall be mine, saith the Lord of hosts, in that day when I make up my jewels."

Now, in this frame of mind, kindly do one thing more. Read again the second paragraph of this chapter, and see if some of the devices and duties (which you passed over so casually in the first reading) now appeal to you.

II. THE NEW WAY OF TEACHING

1. PROJECT TEACHING

"We learn by doing"—that's a familiar statement. But to learn by doing it *together*—that is project teaching. Even gray-heads who hark back to the golden-text days have heard of it. It is fairly new, but as it is now used it is the result of much cumulative experimenting. The fact is, it is not easy, and requires more skill and better imaginative preparation than ordinary fill-and-drill teaching. But the results and rewards are vastly more thrilling.

Let it be added, lest, from a misconception, the conservatives reject this new method, that the project method can accomplish all the old objectives which used to be considered the essentials of teaching—memorizing, facts, stories, moralizing, devotional training—and yet accomplish many other things besides. More-over, these things are achieved better than ever before because they are done with a good will, with interest, and some pur-pose. Indeed, the project method, broadly considered, might be called a way of motivating youngsters, along channels suited to their own age, to do things eagerly which they only did formerly under artificial stimulus.

Let's see if we can make the idea relatively clear and simple —the main idea. The project method is for a class under an understanding teacher. He need not be an experienced teacher, but he must understand and approve of this approach. It works by *group inspiration*, and can rise to high levels of energetic action, with a follow-through that is almost unbelievable. It is indeed perhaps the only way yet employed to solve the grave difficulty of having a seven-day interval between lessons. It is, in a way, not unlike Pentecost and the group in the Upper Room. It produces a new thing, a community of mind and purpose in which the individual is inspired to do something which he never could have been moved to do alone, which, in truth, he never could have done alone. Henceforth the thing he has done with the class is a part of him. He will never forget it, though the details may pass from memory.

It all hangs upon that delightful word "experience." That means something we do ourselves—with our own muscles, our own skill, and—most important—by our own desire and planning. As we get older, clever people in the world cheat us of our experiences, and if we are weak we get into the habit of taking our experiences second-hand. We go to the movies, the art gallery; we read tons of print; we listen to radio actors agonizing over their scripts. We allow ourselves to become the auditors of other people's ideas and performances, and have fewer and fewer of our own. Some day we must resist all these slick exhibitionists—the writers, lecturers, painters, actors, musicians, and first-team athletes—who have taken the stage and are having all the fun. Someday we must become again like children in a class, and respond to a heartfelt suggestion, "Let's do something ourselves!"

When the teacher faces his pupils at the start of each session, they are like cold soup on the stove: the fire has to be lit, and the conglomerate raised to the right temperature. That takes time. Let's repeat that, for failure to grasp this first necessity causes more teachers to fail in the project method than almost any other abuse of it. Remember that your class comes to you (even after a period of common worship) as separate individuals, each with his own present thoughts, tempo, and mood. The teacher has to fuse them into a class quickly, or there will be no constructive teaching accomplished.

Fortunately most of the preliminaries are set, and your pupils readily fall into the groove of the class's established ways. They are a class in outward form, though not yet in mind and intent. The teacher must induce that inward thing, the interest and responsive thinking which will quicken until it becomes the full tide of the class project. When that is in motion, you have attained the warming up, and you can go ahead swimmingly.

But how to accomplish this—that's the problem. Some tips:

(1) Don't reveal what activity you wish them to undertake. Begin your lesson with thoughts that will suggest it, but try to *get them to propose it*—or something like it. Like a committee, the class may often devise something even better. Yet the teacher must act as the helmsman, preventing them from choosing an activity too vast, too expensive or complicated for their ability, time, or interest. Usually the teacher has something well in mind, invented himself, or suggested in the printed notes of his "unit." But the main thing here is to avoid stating baldly, "Now we are going to start making . . . and I have the materials right here."

(2) Approach the activity obliquely, by suggestion, thus: "We have been talking about good manners in church. I heard of one class that made up a little book about church manners to help new people in the Church." Don't add, "Now wouldn't you like to make such a book?" Rather, let the suggestion germinate for a while. They will come back to it, and then it will appear to be their own idea.

(3) Develop interest in a *need*, and let them begin to think how they might do something about it. Thus, a discussion of the need for new hymnals in a mission Church School might naturally lead to the decision to pay for one hymnal, and from that to some way of earning the money. Indeed, many projects, seemingly only money-raisers, can be elevated to the educational level by starting with the object for which the money is to be spent. Discussion of a need always stirs the native

generosity of children, and suggestions for activity are always in order. To let them pass as mere words, allowing no outcome in activity, is to miss a teaching opportunity. All the talking is only preliminary to the activity, which is the real learning experience. This popping up of ideas is the best proof that your directed conversation has been well planned and executed.

When "Let's . . ." or "Couldn't we . . . ?" is heard in a class you may know that original self-expression is about to start. Into what convenient, ready, and effective educational activities can the teacher now guide it? Some immediate outcomes, to use this steam that is sizzling, are these: (You should have them and similar ones at your finger tips, ready for use at all times.)

(1) Send a committee, *e.g.*, to the mission school to report on their need, or to another department to plan a party.

(2) Individual assignments: Find out, look it up, etc. Better have each pupil write out his assignment on a slip of paper to ensure remembering.

(3) Bring from home: old Bible, picture, object.

(4) Get up an entertainment to give someone pleasure (a fine motive), or to make money. Putting on a "show" is frequently appropriate provided the motive is well grounded.

(5) Tell another class: easily arranged, always a good outlet for zeal.

(6) Handwork: Includes all the old things. Many new materials are now being used which are superior to the old crayon coloring, such as flannel pictures, gummed paper posters, and paper bag puppets. But again, do nothing as mere "busy work," but be sure the activity has roots in a teaching motive.

(7) Act it out: Can usually be done then and there, or a show planned for some later day.

(8) Pray for it: fellowship in intercession.

But remember (we say it again, at the risk of being tedious) *what* you do is not as important as *why* you decide to do it, and with what good fellowship and common purpose. You won't need attendance devices in the school where activity teaching is properly employed. You can't keep children away.

2. PRIMITIVE DESIRES

A class was observed earnestly working, copying something from the Bible into some pretty red notebooks. The teacher explained, "They are copying the Christmas story from St. Luke in manuscript style." She added, "I told them they could have the books, for their own, to take home, if they did it without a mistake." That teacher knew her pupils—or rather, she knew humankind. For she had appealed, in the same enterprise, to four basic human urges: to know, to do it with your own hands, to win approval, and, finally, to possess something. If we add the desire to serve, we have the full cycle of human primitive motivation.*

Every child, unknown to himself, yearns for the personal experiences mentioned above. If all goes well, he will find right expression for all of them, throughout his life. That will be, literally, his education. Desire surges up in every heart, and what we desire, we do. When a delinquent boy was asked by the judge why he had done it, he was only able to say, "Well, I guess it was. . . . just because I *wanted* to. There wasn't any reason."

The religions of the East try to erase desire. Subdue and banish all desire, and your struggling heart will be at peace. But who wants that kind of peace? The Christian religion knows Man better. The lusty peace of the Christian life is not

---

* A slightly different listing is given in the next chapter of this book, where *adult* interests are given.

stagnation, but the teeming poise of many vigors. It is a way for the right use and direction of our God-given human desires. Therefore, as teachers, let us understand these desires, and learn how to employ and direct them. They are the stuff with which we deal, the raw materials we are to shape into the finished product. Indeed, I venture to say that the clue given in this chapter may change your whole approach to teaching.

There are, then, five main motives operating daily in the lives of all living persons. Why do people do the things they do? Because something from within them moves them. It would be wonderful if we, as teachers, could say to our class, "What would you *like* to do today?" and then let them do it, while making it an educational activity. The difficulty is that these raw desires are present but unformed. To bring them to light, and provide worthy forms for their expression, is our teaching task.

(1) *To know*—Curiosity makes us look about us, explore our world, make experiments, investigate, ask questions. That is why children—and most adults, too—must handle everything. The baby discovers he can drop his spoon from his high-chair and that somebody picks it up again for him. Thus all normal people want to know more and more, up to the scientist and the world explorer. This joy of exploring must be satisfied, but not dulled by thoughtless friends.

If people find pleasure and success in their first explorations, they may have a long life of constant learning. The teaching clue here is: let your pupils find out for themselves. Stir the desire, pique the curiosity, but don't spoil it by *telling* them. Your job is simply to get them into motion, that is, to inspire them into finding out. You need not—often cannot—go with them on their journey. When you have started them on the search, your part is over.

(2) *To do it yourself*—"Daddy," says the small boy wistfully

on Christmas afternoon, "When can I begin to play with my electric train?" And daddy rises from the floor, suddenly realizing that he has been following a primitive urge to do it himself and has appropriated the toys. He is not childish, but very human. Indeed, thousands of white-collar men are now finding great joy, long denied them in office work, in making things in amateur workshops, with power tools.

This is an urge as wide as life. It includes every form of human achievement by individuals. To be deprived of such self-expression is to have a thwarted and undeveloped life. At different stages it includes handicrafts, the arts, music, writing, sports, and every other activity done for the sheer fun of doing it. Every person has felt it in some degree. It includes two elements—the deep satisfaction of the act of doing it, and the afterjoy of seeing the work of your hands complete. Mine! I did it! There is no glow quite like it.

(3) *To be admired*—To want recognition is a right and normal human desire. Naturally we resent and are hurt by contempt, scorn, ridicule, and criticism. We yearn for approval, for praise, for appreciation, to be noticed, accepted, and loved. Every skilful leader knows how to play upon this universal desire. Flattery is its lowest form, but at its best the teacher employs it by giving deserved recognition. It is not so much the particular words spoken in each case, but the whole attitude. The teacher who genuinely loves his pupils sees their crude struggles, and lets them know he appreciates.

(4) *To possess*—It is natural to want to own the things you use. Behind that urge lies the instinct of security. It builds all the houses, gathers the harvests, makes the collections, amasses the millions, all over the world. The boy saving stamps, the student rejoicing in his rows of books, and the farmer loving his own rich acres are vibrating to this same instinct. While children are communal in some of their early stages, they are

increasingly possessive, and this instinct (often tied up with the motives of achievement and recognition) is readily used in teaching.

(5) *To serve*—It is true that children are, in their earliest years, instinctively selfish, but this is so because they have had no experience of the wishes of others. Presently, in their experimenting, they find that doing things for other people is not only a form of pleasurable activity, but that they are praised for it. They have given pleasure, and their reward is thanks (appreciation). Happy the child who passes through this early stage under loving and understanding handling, and enters social life (in kindergarten) unthwarted in his experiments at doing kindnesses.

This urge is, perhaps the most subtle of all the five, the most easily checked and wasted, and yet the one on which the whole process of Christian living ultimately builds its triumphs. We must nurture and provide outlet for this fragile, deep root of all unselfishness and sacrifice.

But a fearful caution must be added here: any of these primary instincts may turn sour. From being given for our good, they may readily turn to our destruction. Not only all the virtues, but all the sins, are rooted in these raw impulses. Just run over the above five rapidly:

(1) Curiosity may lead to wrong exploration into forbidden territory and to experiment with appetites and experiences made for creative purposes.

(2) Personal activity may turn into the lust for sensation, for novelty.

(3) The hunger for recognition may lead to all kinds of false display, and produce the show-off, the exhibitionist, the braggart. Or, inverted, it may result in excessive shyness or oversensitiveness.

(4) The desire to possess may degenerate into greed, seen

in the extreme of the miser, or selfish possessiveness over husband, wife, or child.

(5) The suggestion to serve may all too readily become a form of vigorous activity, for the satisfactions of doing and being noticed, while forgetful of the real needs of the recipient.

How the skilful teacher uses these five desires is told in the next chapter.

3. USING THE LIFE FORCE

You have probably said, at some time, "If we could only direct that boy's interests into the right channels!" When energy has been spent in mischief, we see too late what we might have done. The great desires of the human heart must be satisfied, and to cause this is the work and the rich opportunity of the teacher. The five persistent desires of life, which we outlined in the preceding chapter, are always demanding expression. We do not have to create them; they are there already. The fire was long ago kindled under the boiler, and the steam is "up." Each separate urge is an opportunity of the teacher.

Let us run over the five, examining each to see how we can employ it in our teaching:

(1) *Curiosity*—We do not have to plug hard facts into unwilling heads. Induce the pupil to set out on his search, and he will make the facts his own, in his own way. The rule here is: Don't *tell* them; make them want to find out. And then don't make the search too difficult. Here are some teaching devices:

Give assignments, asking for reports. Often a lesson may begin with, "We'll start by hearing John's report on what he discovered about the number of missionary stations we had in the Philippines." In preparing every lesson, jot down on small slips some items like this to be given out in class. After a while they will begin to ask for them, and you will see more and more possibilities, and will invent them readily. But these things must be thought up in advance, and written out, all ready to "sell."

Here is the way one teacher managed these personal research assignments. There was a card on the wall with enough lines for every child, and a few columns at the right. When a pupil first accepted an assignment, his name was written on a line, and the date in the space after it. When the report had been made satisfactorily, on some later Sunday, a small star was pasted on the space. No one had to take an assignment, but the publicity of more stars worked readily.

Don't spill all you know. Hold back something. Say, "I wonder if any of you know how boys and girls dressed in our Lord's day. Where could we find out?"

Answers to such questions will be found in Bible dictionaries and in other books in the rector's library, (which is generally somewhere about the church) or at the public library, or by asking some person. Often a question is made up as a direct reference to a certain book, as: How did ancient people think the earth and the sun were arranged? [Clue—see the article "Cosmogony," *Dictionary of the Bible*, Hastings, Vol. I, page 503. Make a copy of the diagram.]

This is one value of the workbooks, if intelligently and ingeniously edited, and as intelligently used. The pupil is set on a minor search, and the place to look is indicated. But if it is always in the same form, in the same place, it palls.

(2) *Achievement*—This must not be allowed to degenerate into mere activity—even though that is better than passive listening. Here is a wide-open field for inventive genius. The activity must be suited to the limited space, time, and abilities

of the class. It must have some real relation to the subject matter of the lesson.

The devices for classroom activity have hitherto been very limited, and some of them have been worked to death: coloring printed outline pictures, or crayoning on colored paper; scissors for cutting outlined pictures; sewing outlines on cards with holes punched; pasting in scrapbooks; making posters. Won't somebody discover some new materials for class?

Some leaders have borrowed from the art departments of the schools, bringing new materials, but not always applying them to the religious field. There has come finger-painting, paper tearing, and even brass-punching, *papier-mâché* molding, and plaster-of-Paris casting.

For older pupils there is always the notebook or the work-book. Add to these such special writing as a letter to a missionary child, reports of a visit or search, original prayers, verses.

The main requirements are these: First, the thing done must be worth doing, so that it gives some pleasure in the manufacture as well as pleasure in showing afterwards. Second, the work must not be too difficult, so that the results are poor, or so that the job is left only half done, never finished. It must reach some concluding stage where it is definitely taken home with approval, or exhibited. It is not necessary that every child make the same article, since some are so slow and unskilled, or irregular in attendance. Often groups of two or three do better, and produce results. For this, one aggressive child, teamed with one or more slower ones, seems to work. Even though the slow ones do little of the actual work, they have the feeling of sharing in the achievement at the end. This sensation of accomplishment, of success, is important.

But a third requirement is that the work call out the imagination of the pupil along the line of the class topic. To appreciate an oriental home, he makes a model of it, arranges its furnishings. To stress service, he makes or does something definitely helpful to certain people. By a variety of motions— making, copying, carrying, packing, acting, finding, reciting —he passes beyond the mere words of the class period to having an experience in his own muscles. This will be a part of him forever.

(3) *Recognition*—Not mere vanity, but natural instinct, requires that we experience some response from our efforts. Encouragement is wine and tonic and food to the soul; ridicule and scorn make us wither and decline. To be forever belittled, criticized, overlooked, ignored, or taken for granted can only cause a thwarted and undeveloped life. Let the wise and loving teacher use these methods frequently: Praise every act, by the standard of the pupil's own ability. "That's lots better than you used to do, Henry." Be specific in commending: "I like that line, it's neat." Draw the class into it: "Look, everybody —how beautifully Helen has pasted this!"

Exhibits, at the conclusion of a unit, are a fine way to call attention to successful work and produce words of appreciation from adults. Children should be near the display, to hear these, and to share by explaining their work.

All marks and grades are forms of recognition, as are attendance schemes and awards. Not enough is made of memory achievement, which often requires great effort. But always let the teacher remember, with imaginative insight, how much shy children need to be drawn out by praise, and be unsparing in the constant word of appreciation.

(4) *Ownership*—There are certain things we want every child to possess, for his very own, at the right stage of his life. These include pictures, prayer cards, leaflets. (It is a sound policy of the Church School to give every pupil *something to take home* every Sunday.) Each should have his prayer corner, gradually developed with kneeler, devotional books, cross, pic-

tures, etc.—best if he has made it himself, arranged every article. Eventually every person should have his own Prayer Book, communicant or devotional manual, Bible, and his personal shelf of religious books, growing through the years.

At the church, sometimes a chair is assigned each child for his own, with his name on it. So, too, there may be personal boxes of crayons, folders for one's own unfinished work. Every article sent home, including the weekly leaflets, should bear the name of the child. When we give a prize, it is not only recognition, but it becomes one's personal possession.

There is something stimulating and steadying about ownership. It produces a sense of importance, of confidence. It gives a deep satisfaction which leads on to other accomplishments.

(5) *Service*—Said a clergyman, "I want every child in this parish, at some time in his life, to help deliver a basket of groceries or toys to a needy family." Granted that such charity may be deemed too shortsighted, and that suitable recipients of baskets are harder and harder to find, he was still correct in stressing this educational experience. It works, as no talk can.

"I'm sure I got my call to the ministry," said a boy from this same parish, "by delivering Thanksgiving baskets. I saw folks who needed to be helped, and I was the one who was helping. It *got* me, although I didn't realize it until after years."

The delicate urge to be helpful does not grow by mere preachments. It thrives only, and most readily, by real acts of service. In planning the lessons over a period, every wise teacher determines to provide some avenue of expression through helpfulness. Fortunately the idea is held by many groups today, and it is possible to find many forms of service experience already going, which may be joined or copied. Much missionary action is of this sort, and develops this instinct to help. The teacher's duty is to see that each child has several of these experiences each year. Little comment is necessary. Indeed, the less moralizing the better. When you have done a kind action, you know that it is right, and the lesson is etched into your memory, woven into the fibre of your being.

These five instincts we work upon, then, singly or in combinations. This is what we mean when we say that we are teaching *children*, not just subjects, facts, and lore. Keep these five in mind, and watch how it makes your teaching more effective, and more fun, when you develop them.

4. ABUSING THE PROJECT METHOD

The rector of a neighboring parish was proudly showing me around his parish house. He waved at some figures above the moulding and announced, "This frieze is a project of our Eighth Grade class," and paused for me to marvel.

There was a complete border of characters about two feet high, all in vivid poster colors, forming a continuous procession of Bible figures. It was really very beautiful. Over the mantle was the Nativity. From one side (starting with Adam at the kitchen door), ran Old Testament people, whom the rector glibly identified, like a guide. In the other direction, past the door of the parish office, strode men and women of the New Testament.

"It isn't quite finished," he explained. "This last space is to contain St. John dreaming on Patmos."

"Did the teacher and class do this alone?" I asked.

"Well, of course, they had help. The children made some figures at first, but they were so crude we finally had to get the art teacher to design them. The children just traced them on."

"And I suppose it arose from the studies of the class?"

"Well, in a way. We were getting toward Christmas, and the Nativity over the mantle seemed a good idea."

"It was their own idea?" I persisted.

"Not exactly. I visited the class one morning and told them I thought it would be fine for them to do it."

"But the teacher was in on it. You had worked it out with her first?"

"No. In fact, she was a little difficult—didn't catch the spirit for several weeks."

"Then I am sure the children accepted the plan joyfully and began to invent ways to carry it out."

"I'm afraid they weren't very enthusiastic—at first. These ideas have to grow, don't you think?"

I agreed. "But the class gradually developed the main idea— about everything leading up to the Incarnation, and flowing from it—and all that," I continued.

"No," admitted the rector, as modestly as possible. "That's my idea. I preached about it last Christmas."

"When they finally got to work," I persisted, "How long did it take them?"

"Oh, they didn't get it done that Christmas at all. We did some work that winter, and during the next Lent. Then the art teacher, Miss Murchison, began to make the sketches. We had to paint over the first ones because they didn't match. Lovely girl, Miss Murchison—it quite converted her—a by-product, if I may so say, of the project. She's to be in the next Confirmation class."

"The children painted them on the wall—naturally?"

"Well, partly. They were not very skilful, and so slow. Miss Murchison did a lot of it herself. She worked all that summer, and into the fall. The new Eighth Grade class recognized it as their project, and were keen about it."

"But you did have the entire class doing something?"

"That was my plan, naturally. But several of them lived so far off, and some lost interest. As in all of Church life," he intoned, "the faithful few stuck."

"Just how many?"

"Well, two. One boy who was quite artistic, and a girl who is awfully good with her hands."

"And they will finish it?"

"To tell you the truth, I have just employed an advanced student from the academy to do this last part. Deserving fellow. Discretionary fund, you know. People were beginning to criticize."

I didn't have the heart to disillusion my friend, but let us consider these points:

(1) The alleged "project" did not arise from the class theme or interest, but was arbitrarily assigned by the rector, and later developed by him.

(2) The teacher was only half-hearted, did not assist in the launching or the growth of the plan.

(3) The art teacher did all the creative work. Indeed, she got the only good out of it.

(4) The project was too ambitious, calling for too great skill, expensive materials and prolonged work. It was never finished.

(5) Instead of being a joyous adventure, it became a job to be done.

(6) It employed only the skilful, failed to hold the others.

(7) It was not done for any felt purpose of service.

(8) There was no culminating class experience, such as a public dedication.

Yet the main idea was good. Here is a better way, done in another parish: Starting about Thanksgiving, the teacher built up the desire to decorate the parish room for the Christmas party. The scheme of figures grew out of class discussion. Being familiar with making posters, they decided to use long strips of poster-paper for background, and made a list of the Bible characters to be done, requiring only that each be twelve inches high. Each child chose two characters. The making of them took two Sundays in Advent. A third Sunday was spent in pasting all on the background. In one afternoon just before the party, they all fastened the strip in place around the room. At the party, attention was called to their achievement, and one boy explained it to the company. That was all.

But that class had employed the project method correctly, and they will never forget it.

5. WORK FOR RESPONSE

Criticize this statement: "Within four sentences the teacher should have a response from the class—some one speaking up, or some one reacting as he has anticipated." Yes, one teacher says he gets too much response, too much talk, too many hands raised. But more of you will admit that you start on your lesson, make your opening statements, even start your story, and still they face you in complete silence. And eventually you know from experience, that this prolonged silence will soon break out in restlessness and some annoying noise. Their minds have not taken hold of your words. As a fisherman throwing the wrong bait in the pool, the fish have not been tempted, have not risen.

Getting the fish to rise to your bait is one of the most illusive of the arts of teaching. Experts may have sold you the prepared bait. But there is no substitute for the skill of the fisherman, his decision of the right moment, the right touch, the day, the light, the change of speed, the trying of other lures. It calls for vast skill, learned through much experience, much patience. And eventually, like all old fishermen, you will wind your own flies, rig up your own tackle. This is only a way of saying that the teacher *is* the course, that all helps, guides, texts, and materials are only good in trained hands. No machine has yet been devised for teaching. Yet some publishers would imply that their courses are fool-proof, can be taught by inexperienced teachers, will unfailingly bring the results you desire. Believe this if you are lazy, and hope to buy results with gadgets. But the sooner you are disillusioned, the sooner you will be an effective teacher.

If teachers would only fix their minds on the goal of stirring each child into his own thoughts, intriguing native curiosity to start on its own adventures, most lesson preparation and procedure would be far different. We must work to stir, to interest, to start processes going beyond the minutes of our class period. If we do not, there may be outward calm and "good discipline," but inwardly there is stagnation, and no real teaching is being accomplished. Nor must it be only of the few alert and extrovert children who give the appearance of class response, while the rest are untouched. Every pupil must be awakened to his own proper activity.

This is the challenge of teaching. We must always try to reach the unreachable, interest the dull, inspire to his own best the brilliant. It puts upon us the duty of meeting their minds, touching them into response. At that point, and only at that point, can real teaching begin. All leading up to that point is only preliminary.

You should plan your opening very carefully. With some teachers this approach is instinctive, but more have to acquire it by experiment, until it becomes a habit. A good opening, which successfully catches the interest and holds the attention of your children, is usually very carefully thought out, even rehearsed. The following are some examples of good openers:

"We are going to learn today about a farmer who became a king. He was a very tall man. What are the advantages of being tall?" (Note: The *coming* lesson takes the stage—not the effort to "review" last week's lesson. Why? Because of the seven-day gap between, during which many vital experiences have occupied their minds. Then, a common experience is used in the first touch of characterization.)

Try a challenge: "How many of you would like to help the rector with the Christmas party?" (Note: If used on a "cold" idea, where no former interest has been aroused already, this will not go well. But if the topic is already on their minds, the response will be immediate.)

An immediate experience: "What did you notice about the altar this morning?"

To catch the class dullard: "John, have you a good imagination? Then let's try it out. Can you see the picture of your own front door? How many steps lead up to it?" (The others are all listening, doing it, but poor John, who never answers quickly, is being given his chance. The satisfaction he experiences may, conceivably, begin a change in his whole life-pattern.)

Give a hint: "We were talking about a man who had a dream —who had a beautiful coat—who had ten brothers. What was his name? (This is better than demanding that they recall abruptly a preceding lesson. Get the old line of thought going again, and they will soon be remembering all of it.)

Yet in spite of your skilful approach you still know that there are several kinds of pupils who respond differently, according to type. Some would argue that we can do little or nothing to change the mental ability and learning response of our pupils. An "A" pupil will always get A's, and a "C" pupil always C's, or in that neighborhood, and there is little you can do about it. Many teachers know that they can almost mark examination papers without reading them, so certainly will each pupil fall into his own established level. Whether this be true or not, we know that we can classify the immediate response of pupils into four types:

1. The slow-witted, who distrust themselves, are always left

behind by the others, who seldom enjoy the developing experience of self-expression, and the satisfaction of successful achievement. If only such had a loving and understanding friend who could get them started.

2. The volatile, who respond too quickly, always have their hands raised, but who forget as soon, miss the real point.

3. The over-privileged, the bored, who have heard it before, and whose many interests and experiences leave little room for the new.

4. The normal, who make up over half of our numbers and who run true to type, to their age and expected interests. This group will include a wide range of mental brilliance, but from them we get our normal outcomes, and build with them a happy, cumulative class experience.

These are the four soils. If you don't believe it, look up our Lord's description of them in the parable: the rocky, the shallow, the weedy, and the good. Or, if you prefer to be called a fisherman, you will follow the wisdom of the old verse:

> Be sure your face is toward the light,
> Study the fishes' curious ways,
> Keep yourself well out of sight,
> And practice patience all your days.

6. THE DIRECTED DECISION

As a boy I acquired a book, *How to be a Magician*, which started out each section with the caption "Effect," and which went on to describe how a dove appeared to come from a locked box, or whatever. Then followed the delightful section headed, "Modus Operandi," telling in detail just how to do the trick yourself.

One such deception I can still manage (provided the audience is polite and not too wary) is the trick of causing some one, apparently by his own volition, to name the top card in a deck. There lies the deck, untouched by the magician. The victim names the card, himself lifts it from the deck, and is astonished to find he is right.

Modus Operandi—Magician (who in advance has taken a peek at the top card; let's say he *knows it is the deuce of spades*), asks victim to mention two of four suits. If the reply is hearts and spades, he asks to choose between spades and hearts. (But if the reply is diamonds and clubs, the magician would say, "That *leaves* hearts and spades; which of these do you choose?")

Next, "Which do you select, deuce through eight, or the upper cards—nine through ace?" If the reply includes the deuce, the magician asks which half of the lower numbers; but if the upper cards are named, he says, "That leaves the lower cards," etc. Finally you get down to two cards. "Of the deuce and trey, name one." If you are lucky, he will say, "deuce," whereupon you ask him to turn the card. But if he says "three," again you have to say, "That leaves the deuce," and invite him to look. In working this trick one frequently gets a series of breaks whereby the victim, at each point, makes the decision toward the card, and you can go on. In any case, he will not be apt to notice how you have directed the selections.

Now, let's apply our lesson. You are having your monthly teachers' meeting. At the start, the rector says, "You will notice that I have a portion of the black board covered. I have written there something which we will look at later in the evening."

He then explains that we are to practice just how to launch a new activity. "You teachers," the rector requests, "will please pretend that you are fourth grade children. I will be the teacher, and I want you all to talk up exactly as you imagine this age pupil would react to my words. All set?"

"When you are sick, do you like to have people send you presents?" The "pupils" recall several personal experiences of being sick. The talk is soon "running along a line" and there is a group mind created, focused on being sick, getting toys, the appropriate kind.

"Wouldn't you like to send something to a child who has been sick for a long while?" All agree, but nobody knows of any such invalid at the moment.

"Did you ever hear of the children's ward in a hospital?" (If the rector is lucky, as in the card trick, some one will have mentioned this before he does.) They discuss this.

A local hospital is soon named. Again with some luck, and some suggestion, some one proposes, "Couldn't we make something for the children there?" The rector doesn't propose it, but plays around the idea until a voice from the class does. This is fundamental to the whole method: *Don't tell them; get them to say it.*

Finally, by the same direction of discussion, it is decided that scrapbooks would be good, that they should be on cloth pages so they would last longer, and that there shall be one book full of dogs, another of airplanes, and another of boats.

Here the rector ends his demonstration by requesting somebody to uncover the blackboard, where it is found that there had been written, "Make cloth scrapbooks for children in St. John's Hospital: dogs, boats, airplanes."

The teachers get the point. Then the method of directing responses by suggestion is reviewed and practiced. The meeting finally summarizes their discovery in these words on the board:

Know in advance approximately what you wish your pupils to attempt. Direct the discussion until they are eager to do something with a common mind and decisive action.

7. INCIDENTAL LEARNING

"We didn't accomplish anything on our lesson today," one teacher told me. "They talked about other things, and I spent all the time explaining." She was very conscientious, and felt that she had failed.

If a class often gets out of hand, and the children insist on talking on everything but the lesson in the book, it may be a sign that the teacher is weak. But it may also result from the fact that the teacher is sensitive to the chance remarks of children, and allows ideas to be developed in the free play of class conversation. Often some vital topic, arising from an event in the community, may call for the first attention of the class that morning, and turn out to be an opportunity for some exceedingly profitable teaching.

Thus, a local youth had murdered a man in a most unreasonable and brutal manner. He was known to the children, and had been an inactive member of the young people's society in another church. They wanted to discuss it in class: What made him do it? Why he had been so "dumb" about not hiding the evidence? What a small sum he had gained for taking one life! How terrible for the families of both! What the young people's society must feel! and so on. The teacher wisely allowed the theme to take the time of the class and eventually developed some constructive class opinions: Was he too lazy to earn money honestly? Had he ever been taught the meaning of the commandment about murder? Was he a mental case, or was he really a bad boy underneath, although he attended church? Had he planned it for a long time? Could he be cured by ten years in prison?

These children had faced, very close at hand, the reality of murder, and had looked, under adult guidance, at a dark corner of human life. Fortunately, this teacher had the wit to recall the New Testament references to demoniac possession, and our Lord's miracles, and was able to find a passage on this. Meanwhile, the time had been spent, and the planned lesson had to be deferred. But who can say that this class did not have a "good lesson"?

Frequently incidents will occur right in the class circle which call for instant attention, and perhaps develop real teaching possibilities. Thus, a tussle in the corridor just before class results in two boys angrily glaring at each other. Or, one may start kicking another under the table. Often as not this last may be simply teasing. The teacher has to make some quick adjustments, or the whole temper of the class is spoiled and the time wasted.

What shall the teacher do to "save the day"? First, he usually has to make a very vigorous and authoritative move to break up the prevailing tone. He commands a change of seats. He speaks sternly, or at least positively, to each offender. To restore the class tone he says, "I won't have it in my class." Teachers who thus act quickly, usually solve the immediate problem, and are able then to get back to the planned line. But it is largely a physical achievement, and only a strong and "strict" teacher can accomplish this.

A teaching way is to grasp the disturbance as a call for group control. "Shall we allow George and Eddie to take part in class this morning if they feel that way?" Then, perhaps a lesson on teasing, how mean it is, how we all hate to be teased. Should everybody try to punish people who tease? Or, on the rights of others. Or, on the right to kick back if you get kicked. Perhaps no finished moralizing can be accomplished. But at least a small sample of anti-social conduct found in the very heart of the little community is used as a vivid lesson from life. An immediate problem is (at least partially) solved by the swift application of some Christian standards, and an impression made that is not merely theoretical. At least all have witnessed a vigorous adult Christian (the teacher) meet a problem in Christian terms.

Other problems in group behavior that may arise at any time within the class include the following:

Initials are found scratched on the surface of the newly varnished classroom table. What does the class recommend that we do to the offender? Who owns the table? What did it cost? What are property rights?

A boy's envelope is reported empty by the treasurer, although he insists (at first) that he did not spend the dime.

A pupil is found to have disfigured his textbook by much scribbling.

A child always forgets her assignments, until the class makes a joke of it. The teacher privately talked to her, made her realize that the group disapproved of her thoughtlessness, whereupon she changed at once.

Someone has claimed that almost every form of unsocial conduct may be found in the schoolroom and dealt with as an opportunity for vital teaching. We have all known of cases of theft, lying, discourtesy, cruelty, bullying, disobedience, anger, conceit, destructiveness, slovenly work. Far from being merely an annoyance to be squelched, these are often a call for the teacher's best ingenuity. No short preparation can make him ready for these moments. But years of faithful work with children, and an alert caring for their real problems, will make these emergencies opportunities to be used. For if the class is considered to be a small sector of the Kingdom, where Christ's will should reign, it becomes a wonderful teaching instrument.

8. TELLER OR TEACHER?

This section is addressed to the teacher with the smooth tongue, who thinks he (or she) is a wonderful teacher, but is really one of the worst. This is the person who is a fluent talker, confident and forceful, whose mind is filled with great quantities of information, but whose method is to deliver it to his charges in a stream of talk.

This unfortunate attitude toward teaching is probably due to native temperament. Such a personality may be only the shy person, ill at ease with others, who covers it by the compensation of excess talking. The trait may arise from innate self-consciousness, from simply not noticing or caring deeply for others. It may be revealed (when the truth comes out at the Judgment Day) that this teacher is really a show-off, motivated by the hunger to be noticed and praised. Not being successful with one's equals, one hopes to impress children.

But whatever the motive, it is a subtle thing, and always difficult to cure. You can recognize it in another, whom you readily label a bore, resenting the fact that he never gives you a chance to talk. If you could always remember how *you* feel when the bore is talking, you would never fall into this error when teaching children, who doubtless have your same reaction, although they have not learned the word to apply to you. At any rate, the result is that lowest form of teaching method —the lecture.

The lecture method may be partly justified when used with college students and others with enough mental content to receive ideas verbally. But even the college lecture is today spiced with the "popular touch" if students are to attend in any numbers, and the popular professor is usually the one who adds a little clowning and hokum, and whose wise-cracks are quoted about the campus. He has, indeed, passed beyond the actual lecture method to the contact method, whereby he actually provokes a response not by his wisdom but by his wit. For laughter, be it remembered by both after-dinner speakers and teachers, is a genuine form of response, primitive and almost universal, calculated to unite groups for a few transitory seconds, and to relax their resistance for further attention. Yet funny-business is thin fare in the long run, and with children (except in the form of cheer and good humor) is of little use in teaching. And even the college lecturer uses other educational devices calling for pupil activity: blackboard, demonstrations, assignments, laboratory work, quizzes, problems, and research.

The pest we have in mind—and perhaps half of our teachers are temperamentally of this ilk, or fall back into this method whenever they are poorly prepared—simply talks on and on. His sole preparation has been the reviewing of facts, formed into loose sentences, plus some items recalled from his active mind.

Let us pause outside the portable partition and listen. Mr. Talky Teller bangs for quiet and starts. "Today I am going to tell you about the Christian Year. It is a sequence of seasons, each starting with some feast or holy day. The principal system takes us through the main events in the life of Christ each year. A secondary scheme consists of special days of memory, such as saints' days and times of special emphasis or devotion, including Rogation and Ember Days." ["I'm going good," says Mr. T. to his inward mirror. "I sure know this subject. What a teacher these kids have! But I wish they would stop wiggling."]

Assignment: Will the reader please note four things that are wrong with the above? We'll add a fifth: the teacher looks upon the class as an audience.

Need we say that pride and overconfidence are partly the

cause of our poor teacher's way? And partly a lack of imagination—that is to say, of real understanding love for children. Surely he never visited a class in the public schools recently, observing the children busily *at work* learning many things. But more especially he has the wrong attitude toward childhood, and an ignorance of the teaching process. Can you remember being bored by a long talk? Then I ask you to place yourself among these pupils and hear them thinking: "I wish he wouldn't talk so much. I wish he'd stop. . . . What's he talking about? I'd like to say something—St. Patrick's Day . . . last year in our room we made. . . ." But the talker has hurried on, missing every possible point of contact.

If you don't teach by telling, by what, then? Here are some ways that real teachers do it: Have you tried to find what the class is interested in—by discussions, sharing of experiences, ideas? Have you inspired them to look it up, report back? Do you know some of the tried ways of expressing it physically, together? This becomes the project, when fully developed. You can easily invent a game or drill using the information you wish to have learned. Compare patiently with what they know already. Have them write it out in their own words—by putting into verse, into an original prayer, into a letter to an imaginary friend.

The mind listens and receives with a strange device. It is a sticky tangle of experiences in our skull which allows only familiar thoughts to adhere. Strange words come merely as sounds, and are gone with the wind. The old psychologists called this pile of experiences the Apperception Masses. If I told you that, and left it there, hurrying on with my lecture (to rub in my point) you would be as bored as a senior warden. ["He's just showing off. Anybody can use an old book."] But if I used those two big words, twinkled my eyes at you to show I think they are funny words, too and said, "I'll bet you don't know what that means," I would still have your good will and interest. Then I would add, "Those words mean simply *what's on your mind*. When you hear new ideas, you compare them with these old things already at home there. If you have ever done or seen anything like it before, you take the new idea into your head because it is *something like* the old ones. Any friend of my old ideas I welcome as a friend of mine. Now class," I say to you, "What is meant by the Apperception Masses?" I'll bet there will be a dozen hands raised, each eager to give it back in his own way.

All right then—back to another class. The *teaching* teacher does it this way. "I am holding an ordinary calendar. What are some important days on it?" (Christmas, birthdays, etc.)

"What four seasons do we have every year? When does each new year start?" When interest is formed, and response started, and old knowledge has been touched, then the channel is open, and a little new matter may be injected. "The Church has a calendar, too, which might be written right on this one."

Notice not only the different method employed, but the different attitude toward the children. They are real persons, and the teacher is vibrating to them lovingly, every minute. He has thought out much of this, in his preparation, anticipating most of their reactions. He can do this because he knows a lot about childhood, and in particular he knows his sheep. His class is a fellowship. But I fear for Mr. Talky Teller. Between him and his children there is a great gulf fixed. Would he be persuaded if one rose from the dead?

9. KEEPING THE CHILD IN THE MIDST

One hears much today about "child-centered teaching." It is the boast of educators claiming the title Progressive that they aim to deal with the child as he is, rather than to put over on him some ancient theology. This approach starts with the observation that the child is a child of nature, that life arises from within, and that our task is to allow these life impulses to reach their God-intended fruition.

We have all heard sermons at religious education gatherings on the text, "Jesus placed a child in the midst." The conclusion reached is either the progressive thesis above, or more often the broader theme that we should pay more attention to childhood. It should be noted, however, that our Lord on this occasion did not give an instruction on the potentialities of childhood, but used the child as a parable or symbol of the child-like heart, which His adult hearers were urged to cultivate. He then *added* a solemn admonition of our responsibility not to "offend one of these little ones *which believe in me.*"

These last words give us a new thought: The child is our responsibility because he already is a believing Christian. This is substantially Horace Bushnell's thesis in his historic *Christian Nurture* (1863). Our children, normally, have never known anything save Christian surroundings. The *quality* of that Christian life, and therefore its effect upon the child, depends upon the kind of Christians who make up his special circle.

Here is a point of view for all teachers to hold: our Lord put the child, every child, in our midst. We are part of the circle around the Lord. He calls our attention to the child with a solemn warning—better be drowned than fail. What is our teaching program, then?

The child was not forcibly brought into the Faith by some super-induced conversion, as certain Protestant systems would insist. He was born there. He awakes to find himself there, and there the Church School finds him, in the font roll of baptized infants, and later in the pre-school and subsequent classes.

We must contrive never to lose him. Starting at the center

of the Church's life, let us surround him with fence on fence of joyous and purposeful experience. The parish and home should provide so many and such right experiences that the boy or girl will have these as his enduring interests. For what we do, we become.

Make a list of some of the experiences which will hold our children to the Church: praying and church-going parents, grace at meals, and companionship in all kinds of Church life. At the church plant, or starting from it: vital worship services, corporate Communions; classes for study, leading to home study, memorizing, explorations, projects, and many activities of learning. Social life suited to his age: parties, picnics, rallies, excursions, breakfasts, dances, dramatics, and the like. Personal relations, private conferences, informal or planned, with teacher, clergy, or other skilled Christians. Special events: children's mission, vacation school, Lenten services, work and service projects.

A mother listed the following Church advantages enjoyed by her thirteen-year-old son each week: on Sundays, serves, attends class in Church School, with opening worship; goes at eleven with parents, sometimes serves; in the evening the YPF. Then he has Scouts Tuesday nights, and weekday instruction on Thursday morning. Perhaps this boy is doing more than the average, but the facilities are there, to be enjoyed as each child is able or interested. These things, through the years, constitute "Church life." He is a part of it, and it is making him.

In practice, what can the teacher do to plan these experiences? Clearly each teacher should try to relate his pupils to all of parish life, and to produce as many added occasions as may be. He should outline, early in the year, a full and varied program of activities. In addition to the regular lessons suggested by the textbook, do your plans include some of these things—one or two social events, either as a class, or with the larger school unit? Two or three work projects calling for activity outside of the Sunday period? Class worship, either with the whole school, or by planned arrangement together at special services? At least one pilgrimage or excursion together?

At the beginning of the school year, you were given a list of names to be your class for the school year. You found them already *in the midst*, in mid-course of their Christian career. Your part is to continue that life, to hold each one so happily that he will never want to leave.

10. CONTENT vs. METHOD

When I invited her to teach this year she gave the usual answer: "But I don't know enough about the Bible." And I gave her my usual reply: "You know enough to start, and you will know your course better as you study it. But I believe you are ingenious and resourceful, and love children, and I know you will make a good leader and teacher."

It raises the old argument of Content vs. Method. Methods may be barren without knowledge; and the folks who know their stuff are often stuffy—they can't always get it across. *What* to teach is contrasted with *how* to teach it.

What shall we teach? Clearly we must hand on to each generation the truths and experiences which have come to us, through the continuous life of the Church, from the first group of Christians who knew the Lord. This is the tradition, the literal meaning of "hand on." It is found conveniently in the Bible and Prayer Book and in tabloid form in the Catechism. But our first difficulty is that these are adult ideas, recollections, and conclusions. They are not easily grasped by children. The Catechism, reflecting the archaic pedagogy of the 16th century, is as clumsy a tool as was ever placed in a worker's hands. As content, it is quite adequate, but as method it requires greatly to be modernized.

The fact is, the tradition is not merely a lot of words, formulas, but a way of life, a family culture. It is action as well as words. Once we have agreed approximately on the things included in this list (the content of the tradition), the problem becomes how to present all this to our pupils. Here is the need for method. And here we have the real divergence in our two camps. The one starts with the tradition, and seeks to fit it to the pupil in hand. The other starts with a study of the child, his interests, impulses, capacities, and tries to feed an appropriate item of the Faith to each pupil as he can take it.

These two approaches need not be in conflict. The distinction is broadly between the objective and the subjective: what is true outside of you, whether you have grasped it or not; and what you have come to apprehend in your own feelings.

If Church life were perfect, there would be no need for Church Schools. Children would learn in company with all ages, as they practiced the routines of the Faith, just as they learn their table manners, and the other matters of the social code. In the middle ages there were no Church Schools (in the modern sense) because everybody went to Mass together, and all took part in the festivals, fasts, fairs, and fellowship of the Christian community. Church life was the same as village life. You didn't have to learn the Christian religion. You were immersed in it. Method and content met in experience.

Unfortunately, Church life is so imperfect today that we cannot trust that way alone. Children are seldom encouraged to sit with their parents, but must work out their Church life in a separate children's world known as the Church School. This is our chief obstacle. To re-enact or explain the tradition, no matter how thoroughly, is not possible because we have such a weak stream of Church life. The teacher must provide this in his own person. To his class, he is the Church in sample, and his example is the first and most useful tool in his kit of methods.

It is assumed too readily today that Catholic Churchmen stress content, while the Protestant-minded stress method. The charge is oversimplified. It is more apt to be a matter of temperament: a "high" Churchman may present the ancient faith most winsomely, and many a "low" Churchman may be quite stiff and severe as he drills on the content of the Faith as he sees it. Protestants, in the present trend, seem to have shifted their interest to the processes of the human heart—child study, pedagogy, etc. They are like the preacher who, it is said, "had a wonderful delivery, but didn't have much to deliver."

Now, you teachers come in just here. The curriculum of subjects (content) is assigned you for the year or season by the parish authorities. The problem of instilling this into your pupils' hearts and heads is yours. In that spirit approach this year's course and class. First, you must master your subject, know your course. Much of it you will have to learn in detail as you prepare each weekly lesson. Then you have to find the best ways of teaching it.

Apply that to your first lesson. Make yourself perfectly familiar with the facts to be taught, the objective to be attained. Then call out all your best ingenuity to make it winsome and palatable for your particular children.

III. THE TEACHER AS A PERSON

1. HOW CAN YOU BE TRAINED?

A teacher in the parish school asked me one day, "Would you consider me a trained teacher?" The sermon that week had been on religious education, and in it I had stated that we would never accomplish our task until we have more trained teachers.

In the ensuing conversation, the following points came out: A trained teacher is one who has *studied* both modern methods and some child psychology, not merely one who handles children successfully by sheer instinct. A trained teacher knows his materials, not vaguely, but well. He is informed on the content of the Christian religion, and the Church's inheritance. He is a responsible person, always careful not to misrepresent the Church's true position, but taking pains to be sure he presents the Faith, not just his own guess.

Three areas of training are essential, and these interweave and support each other.

(1) *Content*—Teachers must know as much as possible about the thing they represent, the Christian religion. With the youngest children this is less important, since the pupils know very little, and the simplest knowledge of an adult will suffice. But in a few years the increasing quantity of the children's information and experience will quickly put to shame any poorly equipped teacher.

As a character in *The Grapes of Wrath* says, "A preacher's got to *know*!" So must the teacher. Even with the youngest, accurate knowledge is safer than a meager grasp of the material. All teachers realize that they must know far more than they use. It is not just the day's lesson that is in hand, but anything which may be asked.

This does not mean that we must know everything. Children respect us if we say, "I'll look that up." (Better, the child enters into joyous experience if the teacher can propose, "Where could we find that out?" and then inspire the child to bring back the answer next week.)

The content of the Faith is everything that is a matter of fact in the historic deposit. It includes everything in the Bible, Prayer Book, and official documents of the Church. It includes traditions, history, and practices. Such matters are studied thoroughly by candidates for the ministry for three intensive years—and the best clergy never stop studying. Lay teachers need not know as much when they start out, but they can keep on studying, a little every year, and the amount of knowledge they can acquire over the years is surprising.

(2) *Methods*—Without training, teachers would conduct their classes just about as they remember their own childhood. Yet the main points of accepted modern methods may be learned quickly, and with further experience and study a teacher will improve. In particular three arts of teaching might be studied in textbooks: the art of *drill* (including review, memorizing, and organizing); the art of *story telling*; and the art of securing *response*. The last is the key to much of the modern way, and takes many forms: the socialized recitation, with directed conversation; the project, with all its possibilities for creative group activity; and original expression, such as the composition of definitions, essays, letters, prayers, hymns, verse, or even radio script.

All this has been learned by the trained teacher, at least in its rudiments, under some guidance, or by private reading.

(3) *Experience and attitude*—If you have taught one year you will do better next year, and year after year. Some authorities recommend that a teacher teach the same grade, using the same textbook for at least three years, thereby becoming an expert on that material. Such a plan also causes the teacher to deal with a different group of children each year, and thereby to become thoroughly acquainted with the characteristics and abilities of that age. He becomes a specialist, say, in fifth grade materials and fifth grade children.

Other leaders allow teachers to remain with the same group, taking them through several grades. The gain here is in becoming the permanent friend of this special group, in seeing them through an important span of years, and thus becoming their spiritual pastor. In either method the teacher learns through experience, and is trained by real practice.

But the really trained teacher is the one who knows that he can never know enough nor do it well enough, and who is resolved to *keep in training* all his life. To such, the ministry of teaching is an open road.

2. YOU NEED A COACH

Some teachers—let the truth be stated frankly—are little more than Sunday baby-sitters. They tell their friends that they don't know a thing about teaching, but at least they manage to keep the children quiet. The fault is not entirely their own. The rector who enlisted them made a great deal of the fact that he was desperate, that he had to have a teacher for every class, and that just being in Church School was something.

Somehow, in selling them on the idea of taking a class, he had made so much of the need and watered down the performance so much that their whole attitude toward their assignment was trivial from the start. It was without any sense of attack or of opportunity. Moreover, this attitude may easily become the atmosphere of a whole school. The impression gets around that very little is expected of the teacher besides being there, and keeping his charges relatively non-violent without the use of an anaesthetic.

Worse still, the attitude of watchman—and little else—may arise from the fact that, once started, teachers are given no aid, encouragement, or guidance. Handed the book in the beginning, the teacher is left to his own ways. *The way of supervision and coaching* is the cure for this epidemic disease.

In the public schools they now call it supervision, and the office of supervisor is among the most important in the whole system. In Church circles the word "coaching" is being used, and it describes vividly a method and a personal relationship. The boys of the team will do anything for their coach. He watches them in action, and they know it. They work for his praise, will follow his slightest suggestion. They know that his reputation depends upon their performance. Far more than for applause from the grandstand, they do their best for his eyes. No wonder the office of athletic coach is well paid. Good coaches earn their money.

Now substitute "rector" or "Church School superintendent" for "coach" above, and you have a perfect picture of an ideal for improvement through keen leadership. A young priest says that he felt humbled when one of his teachers greeted him, "Hi, Coach!" Fresh from college days, he knew the responsibility of that office, and wondered if he could live up to its demand. And, like a good coach, the priest or other top leader in education must claim his position and work at it. It means that, while he guides the whole school, as a team, he watches the personal performance of each teacher. He has them all on his mind and in his prayers.

Some clergy teach one class themselves, simply because of the lack of good teachers. But this is shortsighted, when it is realized that this prevents him from ever seeing any of the others in action. There is seldom any other person, (except in the large parish) who is capable of observing and advising. The danger of having teachers impose upon him by asking him to take their class while absent is slight. (There should be a regular substitute for every class, anyhow—if possible a second teacher, who frequently attends.) When the rector does, now and then, act as the supply teacher for one Sunday he can learn volumes about the weak spots of the class, its tempo, character, and habits. Next week he can speak to the teacher, knowing better just what is wrong. He will have seen, in class action, the difficult children, experienced the difficulties of heating, light, noise, inadequate equipment.

Coaching calls for frequent talks with teachers, either by private appointment or in groups. The personal conference, or grade conference, is worth the precious time and effort required. If nothing else, such meetings increase the personal relation between clergy and workers, creating a spiritual fellowship and an enduring friendship. What is said at such intimate meetings is not apt to be theory, but the meeting of the immediate realities, the sharing of personal problems and enthusiasms.

A teachers' meeting is much like the "locker room talk" between halves of the game. Here, immediately fresh from the heat of battle, with success or failure just experienced, and still time left to go back and do better, the coach provides the raw material of dynamic athletics. He is, for these few intense moments, spark-plug and dynamo. Each coach has his own way, suited to his temperament, his team. Some are notoriously violent; others are calm or winsome. But no matter how the coach conceives of his duty, at the moment, his is the responsibility to inspire his boys, in his own way, in his own words.

The coach, who has watched the first half play by play, may now stress a weak spot in the opposing team, or blunders they have made. Or he may just praise and encourage them to go back there and win. Tactics, of course, but mostly personal inspiration.

But even the arranged meeting or conference is not the only way. The right word may be slipped in during the intervals of a Sunday morning. "You were telling that story marvellously this morning. And I noticed how much better they were responding to the discussion." Or to another he remarks in passing, "I noticed that you had the workbooks distributed too soon. Plan your opening moments better next week." Or, calling at the teacher's home, he goes over the next few lessons, making suggestions from his wider knowledge.

But what if the rector or other leader does not make such appointments or grasp such occasions—what if there is no attempt at coaching in your church? Then the wise teacher may well seek it for himself. It may be that the priest is only engrossed in other things, has never realized his great opportunity and responsibility in this matter. He certainly is well trained in the content of the Faith and is vitally concerned for its teaching. To him the earnest teacher may well go, requesting his time and guidance. Such starts may lead to much creative fellowship and to improvement in teaching skill. And one such courageous start by one sincere teacher may conceivably start a renaissance in both priest and school. It can be done: it has happened! You are *entitled* to guidance. Do not be backward in demanding it.

Many a fine teacher, who would otherwise quit in discouragement or degenerate into a "sitter," would be saved to the Church if this patient, thoughtful guidance were provided him. No doubt we have been placing all too much value upon complete systems and texts and not enough on the teacher as a person, mid-course in his career (between halves, indeed) and urgently in need of human stimuli or praise, encouragement, and constructive advice.

3. INSPIRING YOURSELF

Seated one day in my study, I was weary, and ill at ease. It was the hour I reserved (or tried to) for getting up my Church School lesson. There I was, with all my materials before me— text, notebook, Bible, concordance, and everything. But I was stuck. I couldn't move. The body was there, willing, but the spirit was cold. I just didn't have any enthusiasm for the lesson. My mind was teeming with several other, more exciting thoughts.

What would you have done under such circumstances? What do you do when you feel stale, and cannot "get going" on your lesson? May I help you to face the problem, and shall we together try to work out some solutions?

In the first place, let's have a look at a wonderful teacher in action—at yourself at your dream best. See him with his class, eager, alert, overcoming minor annoyances, holding every eye, calm, yet dynamic. He has his material well in hand. He knows what he is going to accomplish in the class period. He changes from story, to drill, to notebooks at just the right time. His words move, his questions call up joyous response. The class is not aware of any discipline, but only of a very thrilling time.

The answer? This teacher is inspiring because he is an inspired person. Yes, but what inspired him? One answer is, "His religion." Clearly from the deep springs of a truly consecrated, devout, and disciplined Christian life comes the loving zeal which motivates such teaching. It goes back a lifetime.

That, however, is not our problem at the moment. The problem now is how to become inspired immediately, for the present task. One recalls the advice given to every young officer to the effect that when his men are tired, he should tighten up on his discipline. A little thought and some experience reveals that this is intended as a stimulus to the officer, who is as tired as his men. The key man is the leader, who, under temptation to let down, must yet yield the extra bit of nervous force required to maintain morale. If he fails, the whole show may go to pieces.

The teacher is always the immediate source of dynamic enthusiasm. He must never let down, never be below his best leadership. And that often calls for the exercise of plenty of will power. Most of the time, in ordinary teaching, the teacher must inspire himself.

Imagine it to be possible, just at the opening of Church School each Sunday, for the superintendent, rector, and all the teachers, to get together in a separate room for a brief pep meeting. The top leaders would inspire the rest, and all would come out of the meeting, like a football team from the locker room, full of fresh determination to make that class period a success, to win another victory for dear old St. John's.

But since this is not done, it remains for the teacher to inspire himself. It can be done. Consider other areas of life. We do things we have to do, and warm to them as we go along. We tackle boresome routine jobs by a swift whipping up of our sense of duty, or by making the task seem vital and important.

Here are some ways you can do it, for your weekly lesson:

(1) Think of your pupils, one by one. As you do, you will begin to recall things they have said in class. You will begin to long to bring something for each. It will personalize all your preparation. A glow of affection will begin to possess you.

(2) Think of next Sunday's session as a challenge. You will *tighten up your determination* to make it the best period ever, better than some of the ragged ones you have been having lately.

(3) Surround this picture with the confident feeling of success. We can *give ourselves to moods* by a deliberate act of the will—black, degrading, indulgent, unworthy moods sometimes. We can just as deliberately give ourselves to moods of joy and courage, of kindliness, sympathy, patience, or whatever we have felt we lack. But if you approach your preparation with the old dread, a faint heart, and a sense of frustration, you are one with those who "kept back part of the price."

(4) Work up the sensation of happiness about it. This is fun—a rare privilege! I'm going to enjoy this lesson!

(5) "Come out of your corner fighting." This advice of the referee does not mean, of course, a scrappy teacher, with a chip on his shoulder, but the attitude of attack, of keen alertness. As you imagine the opening moments, think of the atmosphere you desire, of the first word you will say, of your aim for this session.

(6) Renew your vocation. Say to yourself, "This is my *job,* my special part in God's world, in His Church. Just because I am alone, and there is no one close to inspire or even criticize me, I will do my level best."

Thoughts like the foregoing require only a moment. But they make the difference between good and bad teaching. We cannot always be at our best; but we can always be at our post. And we can, by the frequent self-discipline of our lives, do our work without any slumping.

We all need a tonic at times—spring tonic, spiritual tonic. You really know where to find the stimulus you need—in the inner court of your religion. You know that always and often you may meet the beloved Teacher of all teachers at His altar.

From there you go back to his sheep with a new purpose, a new look in your eye. You can, because He wills it. The crusaders of old shouted "Deus vult!" and won against terrific odds. You can adopt the same battle cry.

4. MEETING OUR CRITICS

Fellow teachers, how can we deal with our critics? We are frequently reminded that certain people in the parish are saying disparaging things about the work of the Church School, and it sometimes gets us mad. The trouble is, we seldom get just the right chance to answer them; or, if we do, we really haven't much to say.

When somebody who is not teaching, and who seems to be rather lazy and casual about his Church life anyway, says unkind things about the parish school, or especially about my class, then I'd like to say something. It doesn't seem fair. What does he know about it? If he would only try it for just one Sunday!

Let's see how bad the situation is, and what we can do about it. There are several kinds of objectors, inside and out of the parish. Here is the parent who happens to drop in at Church School on one of the worst days—that time when three teachers were absent, when three classes were doubled up, and there was much confusion. Weeks after, that parent is telling others, in meetings, that the school is just a riot.

The solution, or answer, here, as in most cases, is an either/or —either seek out that person, explain the special troubles of that "off" Sunday, get her good will and sympathy, and urge her to help us "talk up" the School, or forget it, and hope such talk will dry up in face of the increasing success and good report of the School. (There is a third choice: that we work at the root of such a situation, have enough teachers always, and so prevent its happening again. But this is a long-range job, calling for a vision comparable with that of an empire builder.)

Here are some of the remarks we may hear—directly, or relayed to us politely through the rector. Two parents have had tea together and had a nice, long chat. They have agreed that Miss M (that's *you*) doesn't seem to be *teaching* their children anything. "I can't find out a *thing* Betty has learned all year. They just seem to have *fun*." You feel hurt when you hear of it. You can't answer back, because it hasn't come directly to you. For a while you feel indignant, waste a lot of emotional force, and lose some charity thinking how unfair these mothers are, how they never do anything themselves, and so on.

Then sober thought says, "Maybe they are right, partly. I haven't been *drilling* on anything. I've been letting the bright ones do all the reciting. I think I'll check up. We'll have a drill, a review, an examination. I'll show them!" That's the spirit: *get in there and teach!*

Here's another, about Mr. N: "The discipline is terrible in his class. I never saw such rude children. If I were in his place I'd make them behave! I'd tell them I didn't have to stand for such behavior. I'd tell them if they wanted me to stay as their teacher. . . ." Sure, sure! Such adults berate the children and blame the teacher for not training them to be Little Lord Fauntleroys. After feeling hurt a little while, you face the answer. They are your children, your problem. You know they have been getting out of hand, and it has both maddened and embarrassed you. You know, down deep, that it was your own fault.

Then there are the parents who find fault with your equipment. "You should see the pretty kindergarten they have over at the Presbyterian Church." That's partly the responsibility of the school management, but at least you can provide stimulus for change. You, in turn, can *criticize where it will get results*.

You don't have to be polite to the rector. He can't quit. We recall the lone teacher, who, weary of asking for better things, placed an old, rickety chair at the front vestibule of the church, just as people were coming in, with these words attached, "Sample of chair provided by the vestry for Church School." The stunt rippled through the town, and brought about a survey by the vestry leading to hundreds of dollars of investment and eventually a new wing on the parish house.

The best way to answer criticism is to work up a popular new front for the Church School. For example, the introduction of movies and other visual aids makes everybody hear that we are up and coming. To reach critical parents, the best way is to make them aware that they have a share in the teaching. Send home assignments patiently, and expect results. A mother, once indifferent, sent this note: "Sorry Jimmie doesn't know duty to neighbor. I hear he's the only one who didn't. He will by next Sunday." Now the mother was in the place of criticism, and was fighting back. She was learning her Duty to her Children.

5. PICTURE OF SUCCESS

In that breathless moment when your class is just over, do you sometimes say to yourself, "There! That's over. I got to the bell by the skin of my teeth. I couldn't have stood it much longer!"? Already you begin to dread the same experience a week off.

That night, as you think it over while going to sleep, you decide, "Yet—it wasn't so very awful. Just a little noisy. And it really was my own fault for not having those sheets typed, those crayons straightened—everything perfectly ready." And you then and there solemnly resolve that you will prepare thoroughly for next week, do all that is humanly possible to have one perfect lesson.

Try to imagine this one dream lesson—this lesson that is to be the highest point yet in your teaching career—this lesson which shall leave you at the end with the glow of victorious achievement, with after-thoughts of golden moments—with no regrets, only rejoicing. This lesson in which you will show yourself that you can do it. Here are some of the ingredients, and this is how it might have looked to you in retrospect:

(1) You had it on your mind all through the week; you spent real time on your books, made a complete working-outline. You went to bed on time on Saturday night, and brought your best physical force to your Lord's Day duty.

(2) You were first in the classroom, controlling the tone, greeting each child with a smile as he entered. (On that perfect day there were no absences, no tardies, and no secretary burst in, mid-lesson.)

(3) You called the class to order just ahead of the rising pressure of physical energy, with a real pause for silence, gathered them into one body with the class prayer, said together very reverently.

(4) Your planned opening words caught interest, that day, and you began to get the expected reactions to your leading questions. Your class not only listened to your questions, but responded. They rose to the bait when you said, "How would it be if . . ." and they proposed ways of developing the project, leading to committee assignments, and the happy, full cry of the chase. (What a delight to recall each detail later in the day!)

(5) Then, when you called them back to a swift review

they performed willingly, for you had your matter well in hand and did not drag it out.

(6) There were actually reports from last week, and these did not take up more than their share of the time.

(7) Your new lesson for the day was launched just before interest was jaded, and you presented new factual matter clearly, with a swift summarizing drill at the end.

(8) The class wrote this in their notebook without delay, broke no pencils, did no scribbling. (They were *interested!* How easily it all went! How could there ever be a poor period?)

(9) The class box had everything needed, and no pupil had to be sent foraging for anything.

(10) You used the closing moments for a jolly new drill in the form of a game, and the bell caught you going strong, with happy activity, although no inappropriate noise.

As the class left, you had that feeling of success. It was tonic and music and inner uplift to you. You didn't need to be told. Later, in the Church service, and at your night prayers, you thanked God. You knew that you had assisted at a humble miracle, made possible because you had been a worker with God.

Such after-thoughts are the rewards of the good teacher. But they need not be as infrequent as they are. The will-to-succeed, partly arising from the desperation of past defeats, may become a steady pattern. Your whole attitude toward your job, toward your own ability, will change.

Remember, one poor lesson undermines class morale and sets you back by at least two weeks. One perfect lesson wipes out one bad one; but three or four perfect lessons in a row make the recurrence of bad days less and less probable. Why break up the steady stream of success by an off day?

Furthermore, there is the matter of changing the whole

attitude and even career of the teacher. Confidence grows with each fresh success until it becomes the tone and quality of the teacher's whole performance. Many a discouraged teacher who dropped out early because of "those terrible children" might now be a success if, having won through to *one perfect lesson*, he had kept on until it became a joyous habit.

6. ARE YOU OVERCONFIDENT?

There are many shades and varieties of pride, but possibly the most subtle (therefore the most dangerous), is the pride shown in the overconfidence of some teachers. Overconfidence is apt to grow on a teacher after a number of years of teaching the same course, or the same age pupils. He knows he has done it, and he can do it again. "It's easy. Watch me!"

This pride starts in the excellent frame of mind of *confidence*. Past success has shown you that you know how to teach. You have reached a stage where you have few problems of discipline, where each lesson goes through its routine as planned, and your class seems to be beyond the common criticisms. But here is the time to beware.

The very nature of teaching is such that we are apt to take all the credit to ourselves. "I did it. I've got them eating out of my hand. I know this stuff, I've been over it for years. And I know children [you fondly allow]. A few stock tricks and they will pay attention."

In short, such a teacher has come to look upon his little period each Sunday morning as the whole substance of teaching, and the management of that his only task. If there is no untoward violence disturbing the rest of the school, if they keep coming, are joyous and eager, then he has done all that can be expected.

But all this attitude subtly stresses only the outward form of the class period. It ignores the deeper purposes and tests of success. Just when such a teacher has won the attention and good will of his pupils, and might be expected to touch them into deep and vital impressions and response, he may miss his chance. He is so impressed with his own power to dominate the group that he forgets the purpose of that power.

Only a deep sense of responsibility can cure this threat of overconfidence. Getting by is not enough. Having an interested and fairly obedient class is not enough. You must strike deeper. Here is how it works:

You are telling a familiar Bible story. You were so sure you could remember it all: you have known it all your life. You run through the main facts—baldly, clipped, and brief, a neat summary. It is surprising how quickly it is all over. Five minutes. You don't want to go back and drag out all the details, make them chew it over. Yet there remain twenty to thirty minutes to be filled in. The fact is, you had neglected to refresh your mind on all the small details. More damaging, you had failed to prepare, by careful thought, all the possible little points of contact with your children. You were dishing up cold potatoes and wondered why they did not relish them.

Here is where the overconfident teacher is revealed. Having failed to vitalize his old lesson and having used up his raw materials too quickly, he must now fill in with fluent improvization. If we could have dictaphones listening in on the last half of all class periods, I wonder how many of them would record discussions of athletic events, camping, and other matters of interest at the moment, including snap judgments on world events, all unplanned, and with no motive save to "hold and interest" the class until the bell.

It is true that long experience and maturity do give a rich

background which may be called upon at any moment. But there should be the main thrust of the period, the planned and intended response, which cannot arise from the spur of the moment. You have to know what you intend to accomplish this week, in a general way; why you are telling the story at all. Here is where the newer project or socialized teaching keeps the teacher alert and humble. You may get by with old factual knowledge, but you cannot be a leader unless you have thought out the day's plan and are freshly attuned, by an imaginative preparation, to your students' probable response. You are to be a prophet, not by making pronouncements of fact (the lecture method) but by touching young minds alive to digest truth.

The overconfident teacher is really trusting his memory. He has fallen into the easy emphasis on matter and content, and neglects the use of right skill in teaching. (In this, we speak not merely of teachers of children and youth, but of those supposedly top teachers in colleges and seminaries who, knowing their stuff—and knowing that they know it!—spend little time on the arts of teaching. If they would spend more time tuning up every lecture for human contacts, examining chaplains might encounter more candidates vitally interested in theology.)

The cure? A humble embracing of the teaching job—every Saturday night. The old teacher is *tempted not to prepare afresh each time*. He needs to follow St. Peter's urge: "Add . . . to knowledge, self-control, and to self-control, patience; and to patience . . . Christian love."

7. YOUR INFLUENCE IN WORSHIP

As Mrs. R turned to bow to the altar, her action was a perfect drama. It seemed, as I looked, to be "soaked in reverence"—as in another atmosphere. She did it without the slightest self-consciousness or artificiality. Slowly she turned as she reached the midst, bowed, as it were, graciously, without haste. Then erect again, she turned with the same quiet dignity and moved on. But you knew she meant something by it. She told you how she felt about an altar better than if she had delivered a little homily.

The children of her class, who were following her through the empty church, paused in turn to imitate her, and each managed it, nearly, in his own way. The passing of that little group through the empty church, on their way to visit something in the side aisle concerning their lesson, was a little pageant, complete. And it was an example of perfect personal influence.

The unfailing attitude of the teacher toward holy things, shown in the simplest words and actions, is one of the most subtle teaching methods in our book. If you are really reverent, it shows itself, in all kinds of ways.

Thus, a manual may say, "Why do we bow to the altar?" The answer may be printed, "Because it is the place where Christ comes to bless us; it is His throne." You may drill on the answer, get it back again on the written examination, and thus equip the pupil so that he may recall the explanation at some future day. But the realization and deepest feeling of the fact can come only from some person who has come to believe it from years of Christian worship, and who shows it.

We are a wise-cracking generation. We have not only swung far away from a pompous verbal piety, but we talk brightly and cheerily about God. Some teachers seem to feel they must make the faith attractive by making it seem jolly and even funny. There are so many jokes about God and religion that most of us, even in Church circles, have lost all shame about repeating them. Perhaps we want it to appear that we are broad-minded, that we really have a deeper religion. Maybe we shrink from showing our real feelings about God. And maybe—I often wonder—we just haven't any real religion, but have to talk about something.

The incidental talk of the teacher must be constantly guarded. He is on duty to his class not only during the lesson period, but at all hours. His conduct about the church is especially important. Here are some ways in which he should be most careful and unfailing:

Kneel on entering the church, and make private devotions with dignity and without haste. Sit quietly in church, directing children if necessary, with as few words as possible, and these spoken softly. The teacher should have his own pledge envelope ready to place on the alms basin.

He should always use the Prayer Book to follow the service, and make every response confidently, in a clear voice. He should make the sign of the cross at the proper places (if this is the custom of the parish, and the teaching of the rector) but always with a smooth dignity that suggests a felt meaning. The quick dabbing motion of some people in making this beautiful act of self-oblation is often startling, and scarcely suggests reverence.

In brief, we are to set an example, in actions as well as words, of how to think and act about God. There is no way to learn the deep levels of reverent worship, and its graceful and approved ways, except by watching and imitating some one who has acquired them.

8. DISCIPLINE?

So you are having trouble with discipline. You mean, I am sure, that you find the children in your class get out of hand. They are noisy, restless, will not "pay attention," and they keep playing with things in the room.

Last Sunday I saw Miss H (behind a door, as though ashamed of being caught) reading hastily in her teacher's handbook. She had left it in her class box all week. Her class has been very noisy lately, and I know why.

If this has been going on for a long time, it is probably going to be hard to cure. The habit-pattern of the class, under you, is formed. Only drastic steps can change it. If you are having only ordinary restlessness, the cure may be closer than you think. Let's look beneath the surface, get the whole story. Who is to blame?

First, can it be the fault of those naughty pupils? Now and then we have all encountered an extra vigorous, over alert, or even moronic child who has been a torment and trouble to every teacher all through his school years. The rector may have to be asked to deal with such a one. It is seldom a whole class. True, sometimes the group may be so supernormal, all from the same kind of privileged homes, and so intelligent that they may, by their very superiority, be a very hard class to teach. But the blame is not on them; they are an extra challenge and opportunity.

Second, then, the circumstances. Do you wish to blame the lesson leaflets—inadequate, too complicated, too mechanized, too obvious, or something? Yet you know that these have been used by hundreds of others. No, good teachers can use almost any system, and a perfect text (if there is any published) falls flat under an unskilled or lazy teacher. Is the classroom noisy?

chairs the wrong height? light poor? ventilation inadequate? radiator pounding? All these can be corrected, and it is your job, as teacher, to report these, and to keep on reporting until you get them remedied. No one in authority will deny your claim. But if you don't speak up, if you wait until another Sunday comes, you'll have the same conditions—and then who is to blame? Here is certainly a place to apply the maxim, "Don't grumble. Kick!"

Well then, finally, try blaming yourself. But don't say, yet, "I'm just not a teacher. I can't do it. It's getting on my nerves. I quit." Wait a minute. Think of your character, not to mention your reputation. See it through. If you quit now . . .

So, frankly, let's list some of the things that may be wrong with your teaching.

(1) The children were racing around the room, doing stunts, in a riot of noise when you arrived. You know the answer to that one: You should always (not missing even once) *be in the classroom first*, setting the tone and pattern as each one enters. Catch every eye and smile as they enter. They are entering *your* classroom, and your plan and purpose are there ahead of them. If you take part in a chapel service preceding, arrange with the rector for you to slip out of church ahead of the children.

(2) You told the story, but when it was over they didn't say much and you found they were doing all sorts of little things. The more you talked, the more the noise increased. It was like a pressure of steam, just simmering, ready to pop off. The cure? Get up your lesson better. Perhaps you haven't caught on to the discussion method. Read the section in Chapter VI on that. Controlling conversation is one of the highest of arts, but it can be learned, and once you master the fundamentals, get the right attitude, you will begin to get many happy periods. Admit it: you just skimmed over the story,

planned nothing for your class to do, anticipated no outcomes.

(3) But even your planned activity didn't work. When you passed out the notebooks, the confusion started. Why? Perhaps the pencils were broken, dull, or too hard. Possibly you merely dictated some summary or answers. Nothing interesting in that. Merely a manual job, and some children have a real displeasure in writing. Perhaps the loose leaves were tearing out, or the table too small for so many pushing elbows. Remedy that before next Sunday!

The real trouble here is that you didn't provoke any vital desire or reason for writing in a notebook. You commanded, "Now, pass out the books." Better: "How many of you would like to make a list of the things we saw in church—to show to father and mother?" "What new words today can we add to our vocabulary page?"

But you used that word "discipline." That shows you really think it ideal to control children, to have them always quite submissive and subdued, entirely proper and tractable. You still harbor thoughts of the teacher as a disciplinarian. Perhaps you picture the stern schoolmasters in Dickens' stories. Certainly you cannot have in your mind a picture of that constructive, happy atmosphere desired in a place of learning. There is no consciousness of discipline where the disciples (*i.e.*, learners) are touched alive by a loving and understanding teacher.

9. SHALL I TEACH ANOTHER YEAR?

During May and June, leaders all over the Church think ahead to fall. They have two main worries: Who will be on the teaching staff and, what textbooks shall we order?

As for the matter of teachers, there are several points of view to consider: the rector's, the child's, the parent's, and the teacher's. Each has his stake in the success of the school, and each his ideas on the basis of experience.

A few teachers will be tempted to quit, having had a rather unhappy time of it, either through their own fault, or because of the failure of the school officials to be helpful. If they have definitely proved themselves temperamentally unfit for teaching and are having little pleasure or success in it, then no doubt their case will be settled by the rector's not inviting them again. They will not appear in the line-up next fall, and they may be "unwept, unhonored, and unsung." And yet many such a one-year's teacher might be saved for development into an effective leader. He has dealt personally with the problem of teaching children. A new start, a fresh inspiring, another class, and closer supervision and encouragement may yet bring such a one to years of great usefulness.

Then there are the fine teachers, each with his own thoughts. There will be those now rounding out one, two, or maybe five or even twenty or more years of teaching. (The average term of service of parish teachers throughout the Church has been estimated as from one and two-tenths to two and one-half years, although no survey has ever been attempted. The average is brought down by the many casual and temporary teachers.) Into the minds of all teachers, late each spring, the thought intrudes: To teach or not to teach! It's time I dropped out. I deserve a rest. Let somebody else. . . . Then sober loyalty speaks. Shall I offer myself voluntarily, knowing that my experience is now worth something, that I can do much better another year?

Look, then, into the mind of the rector. If he is easy-going, he hopes that events will solve this annual problem for him. The long-time teachers, he hopes, will hold on for one more year. He doesn't dare ask them, fearing they may take the occasion to resign. He does not wish to open the question. The weak ones, he hopes, will start out next fall and do better. Or, if any give notice, perhaps some new person will move into the parish and offer.

This is not an admirable attitude for the priest to have toward this key problem of his school. The alert priest rebuilds his staff every year. He has teachers coming up, through preliminary experiences of assisting, substituting, and reading, for permanent assignment. Each active teacher is approached to make a decision whether to teach or not, and which class. This involves a personal interview with each in the closing weeks of school or the early summer. In the really large parish this may be done by a letter or a phone conversation. But, in any case, if it is understood that teaching is an annual call and that poor teachers may not be asked to continue, then the whole tone of the school is much enhanced. "It's an honor to be asked to teach in our parish."

How does the parish leader keep up his supply of teachers? It is not a matter for a season only, but one that must be kept forever alive. On the ideal plane, teaching is literally the first call, the absolute priority on Christian talent. All other service comes second, and we have a right to claim that a person drop guild work and other activities, if need be, in favor of teaching. The pastor who believes this looks upon every one of his people as potential teachers and his selection of them a high and holy call. He must make no mistakes, but he also must feel confidently that he has a right to call. Such a priest has his list at hand or in mind always. It includes the present teachers, their individual abilities and weak points. It has names in reserve of persons temporarily unavailable this year. There are new people, people who used to teach, parents who should, young people in training.

The skilled educational leader lists his requirements. First, loyalty, zeal, and some real religion. Folks may some day be keyed up to the teaching pitch by cumulative experiences and inspiration, but unless they have already arrived at some high plane of Christian devotion and motive there is no use asking them to teach. Lacking this, they may, indeed, be talked into serving, but their work is doomed to mediocrity. There is no substitute for the motive of love for God, His Church, and His children.

Second, there is the practical point of availability. Some people are not free to come every Sunday morning, for reasons of family or other duties, or health. (For some, an alert rector has found funds sufficient for a baby-sitter, or for a taxi, thereby gaining a key teacher for a modest annual cost. This is not pay, but the removal of a difficulty.) Most of this group will have to be on the inactive or future list. They are kept reminded that they are wanted in the future, and their attitude is, "I'll be back another year!"

Third, there must be knowledge, skill, and experience. This is important, but we are apt to make too much of it. Persons who seem to qualify preëminently by culture and education often make poor teachers. For one thing, they are apt to be overconfident, cocky, and dogmatic. Or they trust too much their imagined great store of Church knowledge, and do not prepare their lessons carefully. The truth is, all teachers, in public schools, colleges, or the Church School, learn their subject as they teach. There must be, of course, the preliminary study, and some general preparation for teaching. But it is a truth for living that we know nothing well until we have given it to someone else. The act of teaching clarifies, organizes and vitalizes what we had before known only in words, or in an academic fashion.

Therefore, never be ashamed to admit that you are learning as you teach. The vital thing is that you are teaching, and doing it from a sense of deep duty, and with the attack of some real spiritual enthusiasm. The clergy are always looking for that illusive personal factor, which may be lying dormant—the teacher instinct. People who are not really loving or gracious never can become great teachers. Ingenuity helps. Good humor, adaptability, assorted talents, nervous force—all these help. But deeper yet is the essential note of a sense of call, a stirring of personal dedication to serve God through His children. If a person genuinely likes children and wants to help them, he can learn the material and pick up the methods.

Materials, methods, motives—these three—but the greatest of these is motives. You *can* teach if you have the inner urge and feel that you ought to. In this frame of mind, will you notify your rector that, if he wants you, you will teach again next fall?

10. ARE WE TEACHING ANYTHING?

The Chaplains say that our men in the service, supposed to be graduates of our parish schools, knew woefully little about their Church. If we ask the ordinary youth some fact about his religion he may give a very wrong or ridiculous answer. Or you may find that he knows the answers with surprising accuracy. It all depends on those who taught him.

Surveys and questionnaires have been applied to find out what we have been accomplishing over the years. And these reveal just about what we always knew: children who sat under earnest, patient, and thorough teachers knew what they had studied, often many years afterward. But those who had mostly indifferent teachers had only the vaguest information about their Church. And this group has been found, sadly enough, to be in the majority.

Teachers must *teach*. If they don't, nobody else will. A single Sunday's lesson may not seem important, but if it slips by without some drill, factual or interpretive, it starts a kind of slow starvation of the pupils' mental and spiritual life.

Next year, when you have finished the season's work with your class, just what will you be able to say that your pupils know as a result of the weeks under you? Before me lies a set of Goal Cards for each of the Christian Nurture Series' years. Here are listed, on one small card, the objectives for the whole year. This is the one for Grade 3, "God With Man." It lists: Say prayers morning and evening. Know the answers to certain key questions which summarize the year's theme. Memorize: a hymn, prayer on entering church. Attend: a service every Sunday, a Baptism, a Confirmation, the Holy Communion. Five pilgrimages to the church. Make: plan of church, chart of three sacraments. Retell at least these four stories: The Great Temple, Baptism of the Jailer, First Confirmation, Lord's Supper. Serve by: weekly, birthday, and Lenten offerings. Keeping books in order in church. Making a class gift.

Here is something to aim at, something by which to measure your efforts at the end. Such a goal calls for patient repetition and drill. And it puts it upon the teacher to accomplish these points in every pupil, rather than make a showing through his brilliant ones.

There are really three kinds of knowledge, all of which are dealt with by the class teacher. These are facts, skills, and interpretations. These are roughly the three columns that used to be listed in the front of the old Christian Nurture manuals, headed Information, Service, and Devotional Life. (Church Loyalty and Memory were the other two, forming the five strands of the strong rope of the Christian Nurture plan through all the years. These two can really be included in the above three, for simplification of thought, for the moment.)

(1) *Facts*—Our first knowledge is identification of the things around us. Children, by some natural curiosity, want to know the names of things and of people. They are like the old farmer, watching his pigs eat, who remarked, "Ain't them rightly called hogs!" So children love the story of God naming all the animals. They learn first all the common nouns.

In teaching, a great deal of time must be spent in drilling on names, dates, vocabularies, descriptions, numbers, definitions, stories, and the like. These are the facts about which there is no argument, and about which you had better be right. They are easiest to teach, and are the lowest level of knowledge. Too many teachers pass them over lightly. Or, in the other extreme, some spend all their time on factual drill. Yet only drill can impress them.

(2) *Skills*—Our aim is to make every child a skilled Churchman. He must know how to perform every Christian act, and by repetition have formed habits that will last into life, exactly how to act in church, and how to use his books. Here should be listed the important matter of drill in finding Bible places. Many adults have never learned about this.

The Christian skills include training in courtesy, thoughtfulness, and practical service. How to behave toward others in church, how and when to say your prayers, how to prepare for Communion. These things are learned in the Church School, under teachers, or not at all.

(3) *Interpretations*—You don't really know anything until it has meant something to you, until you have vibrated to it as a person and made it a part of your life. Here the teacher calls up all the techniques of self-expression: write a definition, a conversation, a letter, poem, or prayer; draw a picture of it, make a model, arrange the parts (sand table), act it out. All activity tends to pass into personal interpretation, giving a sense of vital meaning. So we allow capable children to conduct

class drill, or invent their own questions about the lesson. Interpretation means digesting the matter, and anything that prevents the teacher from merely telling in words helps in this. "Progressive" education stresses this strand almost exclusively.

Let's keep a balance between these three areas. Watch lest you fall into stressing the one kind of knowledge that appeals to you. Above all, be sure that interpretation is based on the facts, and is not just sentimental gush or over-stimulated, meaningless activity.

IV. IMPROVING YOUR STYLE

1. RESERVE AMMUNITION

We frequently hear a teacher say, "I often let my class out early when we have finished the lesson—or at least I used to. I thought it was better than having them make a noise the rest of the period. But the rector told me that it disrupted the school and that I must hold them until the bell."

This teacher had the familiar experience of running out of material. In some way her timing was bad, and, long before the class should have ended, she found herself with nothing interesting to do or talk about. This may be due partly to the *lesson* attitude, which looks upon each period as a separate experience, emphasizing the "lesson for today." The *unit* approach would at once relieve this tension, with the stress on the continuity of a theme, with each class period a continuous stage of the fluid unit.

Yet even with the unit approach we may momentarily run short of material. We have all had the experience. It is still twenty minutes before the bell and the story seems to be about exhausted, or the talk may have gone hopelessly off the subject. You are in a mild panic. What to do now! How can I hold them? They are starting to get noisy. If you dismiss them it would be an admission of defeat. Other teachers and pupils would see your children leaving, might demand to be dismissed. You know this would make you seem inadequate, and would undermine general discipline, as the rector said.

What you need is reserve ammunition—something up your

sleeve that will fit almost any occasion, be useful and valuable at any time. Often it is not a matter of filling in time, but of saving a lame period, vitalizing a theme that is dragging. You have to do something different, and do it quickly. We all know the teacher who does this by talking about football or some other secular subject, merely to "interest them." In truth, many a college student has been enlisted as a teacher with this as his sole and announced qualification, that he could "hold" the boys. Or, we overhear a teacher saying, "If you'll all be good and listen to the lesson, I'll tell you about the ice follies I saw Saturday night."

If we may pause to tear this last revealing remark in pieces, we may note at least four typical and very common flaws in our teaching: (1) "Be good and listen" is an utterly inadequate conception of class discipline and method. (2) The "lesson" conceived as a little handful of material, to be gone over on the given Sunday—and that's that! (3) The entertainment emphasis, and the stress on "telling." (4) The revelation that the teacher had used Saturday night for something other than preparing the lesson.

The principle revealed here is that you must know much more about religion than you are teaching in the unit or course. You must have reserves, ready at hand. Preachers understand this. They must often have paragraphs and illustrations ready in case the movement of the sermon calls for it. They must be as ready boldly to omit bits that might impede the balance and finish of the sermon. What to have on hand that will fit in almost anywhere, is the problem.

Here are some useful things you can have in your bag:

(1) Additional matter on today's lesson. As you prepare, note certain points that might prove too long, that are to be used only if necessary. Having such points on a separate card keeps them in hand, but separate. (This is the great advantage,

far from being a burden, of those courses like Christian Nurture, of which teachers commonly say that there is "too much to cover in one lesson.") For example, you may have some notes on the life of a saint, or some travel background.

(2) Stories: An extra anecdote illustrating today's subject. If you prepare your lesson early in the week, you'll find that your subconscious will go beyond the words of the editor, and you will remember or invent additional illustrations.

(3) Games: These include the published card games on the Church Year, Life of Christ, vestments, "Halleluiah", and the like. There are also some you can play without special equipment, such as finding texts in the Bible (class divided in half; first team to find the text gets point); "My Bible tells about Adam," to which the next one called upon must say, "My Bible tells about B——" and so on through the alphabet.

(4) Clippings: You will see cartoons, pictures, verse which are worth sharing. Learn to put them with your notebook. A fine discussion may arise from one clipping.

(5) Drills: Take Prayer Books, "What comes first, the Litany or Catechism?" Review the catch-phrases for past lessons. You can always remember the policy, "If you have any extra time, *review*."

(6) Objects: A souvenir from the Holy Land, a book, a letter. But have it hidden until wanted.

(7) Visual equipment: If you have the new projectors and slides at hand, ready for showing without waste of time (preferably all set up in another room) they form excellent reserve ammunition. But this is best done as a review of familiar pictures, for pupils to re-tell the stories themselves. (For the normal use of such pictures you will of course have a careful build-up in the class period.)

(8) Memory drills: You can always fill out your time with these. But you may have to learn some methods. Try flash cards,

hand-made, with lettering in large crayon. One pupil recites with his back to the card, but facing the class. The rest of the class check up on him, and so are kept interested. But the teacher must have memorized the matter first! Indeed, one of the smoothest ways of using time is to have the teacher start reciting a familiar passage, asking the class to join in concert, stopping now and then to let an individual carry on alone.

(9) Choral reading: This is described elsewhere, but makes a ready filler.

(10) Dramatics: Easy if you have thought them out. To go through one portion of the story is often enough.

(11) Planning a coming event or project: You'll run 'way over the bell with this.

On this whole matter some general suggestions might be added:

As you pick up these items, salt them away somewhere in your notebook. It becomes a kind of good habit. "I can work that into my class, somewhere." Everything you think or do becomes related to your teaching.

Yet do not strive to bring in new things *every* time. As you grow more experienced your timing is better. But still you will need your reserves unexpectedly. I've saved a particular stunt six months before the right moment came.

Having such reserve material will give you confidence, and you will be thinking of your course between Sundays more and more. Your teaching is not one isolated hour on Sunday morning, but a continuous process, a year-long sharing in the lives of your little flock. If they are on your mind, often, your lesson preparation and your teaching will acquire a depth and a reach. You are in the position of the mother who must prepare meals for her family. You must use forethought to have plenty of materials ready, to make them attractive, varied, sustaining. You wouldn't think of ending without a nice dessert.

2. THE ART OF LEADERSHIP

The teacher is a group leader and should be informed on some of the well-developed techniques of leadership. Early in your teaching there has to come an understanding of your personal motives. At first there is the general enthusiasm to be teaching, with thoughts of being useful and of serving children through the Church. But this vague feeling has some day to be clarified by asking the questions: Why do I desire to lead these children? What do I hope to do for them? Am I really teaching from the highest motives, or just to have another kind of experience?—or to be praised, or what?

But when motives are somewhat straightened out, and you have hit your stride by weeks of fairly successful teaching, you will begin to note certain matters that concern the art of leadership. Some can be taught you, but more you will have to work out as you go along. Above all, you will begin to adopt certain practical policies which will enable you to get better results.

In particular, the good leader in Church work must remind himself frequently that he is *employing people for their own developing experience*, not just "putting over" some stunt or enthusiasm of his own. This is the fundamental educational or nurture principle: that people in order to grow in Christian character must have many varied experiences within the full life of the Church. Not many things are actually necessary to *get done*, but it is vastly important that everybody be led into doing *something*. Those dumpy clay figures, considered as a manufactured product, are worthless, but as vehicles of activity for the third graders who made them, they caused a large imaginative grasping of the Christmas story.

Here are some practical policies for leaders which experience has formulated. *A good leader will always. . . .*

(1) Provide work for the weak. If you always call upon the capable, the show-offs, the extroverts, the enthused-already, your program is not educative, will never help very many.

(2) Use local material. That is to say, don't work up some activity calling for talents rarely found, or requiring a person to be brought in. Build your projects out of the abilities as well as the interests of the actual children you have. The same project will work or fail in different groups.

(3) Expect sacrifice, and ask for it. This applies to older people especially, but even children, as well as their parents, respect a large request. People will come to meetings and rehearsals, if you ask confidently.

(4) Enlist early. The early bird is always heard. People, even children, think more highly of an engagement long arranged and will prepare better for it. In building a long program, people who are asked in October are less apt to refuse a duty in January.

(5) Have a program always. This will most often be formulated in conference with other leaders, or a committee from your group. The highly capable executive type leader is too apt to create his own brilliant scheme alone, thereby missing the educational experience of creative planning.

(6) Provide reasonable novelty. Falling into a groove dulls interest. But if you know that there may be something different any Sunday, it helps to create an atmosphere of expectation. Therefore, alter your teaching order, rearrange table and chairs, or go to visit another part of the church.

(7) Delegate as much detail as possible. The super-leader is not supposed to do things, nor even to get many things done, but to provide pleasant and profitable activities for as many people as possible. Thus, the second-rate teacher (who may really think he is most efficient) will say, "I'll bring the paper

plates, the tissue paper, and the thumb tacks," not realizing that here are three separate assignments.

(8) Think of all projects as means for individual activities. Put in things that call for more labor, not less. Break down each event, as part of your advance preparation, into individual tasks or duties.

All the foregoing applies particularly to the clergy, and other leaders-of-leaders, who are apt to get into the habit of taking the short cut of doing everything themselves. Recall how our Lord let the boy provide the loaves and fishes, and then how He gave His disciples, whom He was training, the experience of serving, and of picking up after.

These eight practical policies, thoroughly learned and frequently practiced by the class teacher, will change his whole attitude. He will be amazed to find with what enthusiasm his pupils take hold of the work, come regularly and stay late. But oddly enough this one line of attack may be the one weakness of which a teacher may not be aware, his blind spot to seeing himself objectively. Many persons, placed in positions of leadership, may be keenly self-conscious of certain inconvenient traits in their own character, such as timidity, resentfulness, procrastination, or lack of zeal. But few realize that they don't know how to *get people into motion on their own power*. Often, they don't even realize that this is their main job, and their supreme opportunity. The technical name for this is "to motivate people."

3. LEADERS OF YOUNG PEOPLE

If you have been asked to lead or assist with the young people's group you had better analyze your job, and make thorough preparation—or else! The *or else* means a year of exasperation, futility, and wasted effort. Possibly there is no department in parish life in which we do such poor work, and miss such large opportunity, as here. The conspicuous youth societies in certain large parishes are generally (if the truth is revealed) only a fraction of the young people available, and they are not the ones who need it most.

No national youth office has ever been able to help very much. The key is the parish leader, the loyal one who, through a year of blood, sweat, and tears, will struggle through with the high school crowd. Therefore, clear motives first, with a firm resolution to give loving, patient, and intelligent leadership. Make up your mind. If you take up this task, you are doomed for failures vast, heartaches, and disappointments. But you will also have unexpected bursts of success, increasing satisfaction of friendship and fun with boys and girls who are going through some of the most difficult years of their lives.

In the typical parish there will be found the unsettled relation between (a) the high school classes in the Church School, and (b) the Sunday evening meeting of the young people. The rector dimly hopes they will all come on Sunday morning for *both* a high school class and one of the regular services. In addition he hopes that they will all come *again* in the evening. But this vague hope is seldom implemented by a workable program, and the three events remain as bidders for the youth's Sunday attention and choice. In practice, each attends the one or two which appeal to him.

The first step should be to straighten out this muddled parish thinking by forming a Youth Council (call it committee, board, sponsors—no matter) to settle policies and objectives and start a program. Persons on this body (which should meet *monthly*, if youth work is to be kept vital) should be the rector, youth leaders, some key parents, and two or three of the young people themselves; in all, five to ten.

The Youth Council prevents the youth program from becoming the sole work of the youth leaders. Here all problems are frankly discussed and solutions worked out. At times, every name on the youth list should be discussed, to decide if the program is really reaching those for whom it is intended. This council will have to see clearly the local need—whether to stress the Sunday night society or some Sunday morning venture, a week-night event, or whether to meet once a month. How often shall we expect them to receive Communion? What assistants will the leaders need? adults for social events? a program director? Just how far can students be expected to be leaders? Do they have to stick to the traditional events and program in the parish?

Yet, beyond the backing and constant sharing of the program by this council, the real work is carried on by the youth leader. He or she has to be forever looking ahead, holding the attention of individuals, thinking of ways to catch the interest of the absent, the slipping. There are the thousand arts of program making, of inspiring and using vitality, of touching natural idealism and clinching it with a religious experience. All the time, there is the problem of holding the interest and securing the attention of all kinds of oddly assorted individuals.

In brief, here are a few items to have in your mind:

(1) *Collect materials,* early and always. You will need new stunts, games, projects, ideas, plans, and your file should be always at hand.

(2) *Remember individuals,* even to allowing time or making a pretext for personal chats. Young people are in a world apart, have few adult intimates, are, underneath their noise, really lonely, hungry, and confused. And they are very sensitive, the toughest ones often the most.

(3) Work at your *whole list*, not just the activated central group who come to meetings. They are all your children, and

the absentees are your wandering sheep, who need you most. If *you* don't win them, who will?

(4) Try everything, hope everything, stick to it to the end of the year. Ask help from other adults, but keep the ball rolling yourself.

(5) A good formula: Work *for* your young people; one step higher, work *with* them; higher yet, try to get things done *by* them. *For, with, by:* each succeeding level is more difficult, and more worth while.

Every society reaches a low point, or dies out, about every seven years. Don't be discouraged. Make a fresh start this year: it may be time for the beginning of a new cycle.

4. YOUR CLASSROOM EQUIPMENT

If this is to be your first year of teaching, you had better check up and find out just what equipment they will provide you at the church. The housekeeping affairs in many Church Schools is a scandal. If you should start to explore in the parish house on some day in late summer, you are quite likely to find articles just as they were dropped the last Sunday of the school in June. The cupboards may prove to be a rat's nest of untidy remnants of crayons, scissors, papers, leaflets, and dried-out paste.

You find the space (it is not likely to be a separate room in most parishes) where your class will meet. You start taking an inventory. It runs something like this: One discarded bookcase (hinge of door broken)—hasn't been cleaned out in years. Teacher's box, with name of teacher long gone. Broken pencils, all styles. Construction paper, many sheets bent, only the dull colors left. Pile of broken lesson sets, going back several years.

If you can get permission to clean this out, you can soon have all this mess out in the middle of the floor. Some of it can be used, but most of it should be thrown away. Don't even try to hold broken lesson sets "for some poor school that might use them." That would be no kindness. No school can use junk. Be ruthless about clearing the deck. We spend little enough on equipment, and all imperfect materials are a drag and a confusion.

Try starting with a clean slate. You have been told that your class will probably have twelve children. Your list starts out: First Grade—12 children. Need 13 chairs, 14-inch. Two tables, 4 feet square, 26 inches high (see catalogs). Blackboard, low. Separate shelf or locker for class supplies. (A triangular corner cupboard, fastened shoulder-high, takes no floor space, means that the class materials are always where you left them.)

Then your list of *new* supplies for the class: Pencils, crayons, chalk, eraser, good scissors, plenty of construction paper, small individual jars of library paste, paste-sticks, rubber-bands, brass rivets, and anything else you think may come in handy during the year. You never know when you may need some equipment, and one shopping tour at the start will save you much annoyance on some later Sunday. And what a thrill to have all these at the opening day, in order, on your shelves. The children will enter into plans for a committee to *keep* them in order, and to pick up after each lesson. They will, that is, if you will it, and keep the idea alive. Class order and tidiness may become a habit, given a clean start. Two minutes, reserved before the closing bell, for picking up, works wonders.

Now you may pause in your exploration to decide if the conditions of your class space can be improved. If there are only portable partitions to shut your class off from others, are these partitions large enough? Could they be rebuilt, made more sound-proof? At least, are they in repair, or do they sag, lean, and look disreputable? Is the room cluttered with gear

of other groups—scouts, guilds, janitor? How about pictures—
have the same old steel-engravings of religious subjects been
hanging there for years? Are there any charts, posters, etc.,
from last year still hanging around? Is there a sand-table in the
corner, littered with cartons, and not used since last Christmas?

From such severe criticism plan your campaign for improvements. Could the room be painted, or a bright wallpaper be
agreed upon by all? Are the lights right, or are fixtures old,
battered, temporary? How about the window shades, the curtains? Thus details grow, and you enquire about the proper
persons to approach for relief. Parish politics may call for big
names, or working through some seldom-activated committee,
but all are self-conscious about criticism of the work for children, and will do amazing things if one vital person keeps
nudging them. Possibly you have already found yourself in the
rôle of a reformer, and your plans have begun to be known
around the parish as "The Program to Renovate and Equip the
Church School Rooms." A total price will have been secured
for all the items, and it will be noised about that "We need
two hundred dollars for the Church School." It helps if it is
told that children, on the average, bring offerings of fully $2.50
per year, (pennies are out—it's nickels and dimes, now) yet we
spend on them less than a dollar per child per year.

The money will come, easily. And with it an opportunity for
making a fresh start throughout the school. Everybody will be
interested. The teachers will rejoice. The improvements will
last for years. Other things will follow. Better secretarial work,
records, system. The teachers are released from petty annoyance
of hunting equipment. True, externals will not change the
problem of vital teaching, but they help.

All this is good strategy, whether initiated by you, the new
teacher coming in like a gust of fresh air, or by the rector. It
will call attention to the fact that the Church's school is vitally

important, that somebody really cares about it. Many older people are filled with sentiment about children (in the abstract) and will give generously, when asked, for "children's work."

The average teacher is usually more concerned with the preparation and performance of his lesson than with his equipment. He should not be asked to take all the responsibility for everything, yet at least he can keep others in authority aware that *he* is the vital figure, and that he must be released from needless annoyance. Teachers have a right to expect that when they arrive at the church the physical circumstances of their class shall be as completely ready as possible. Many a priest who says he "just isn't any good about the Sunday school" can at least know how to order materials, and insist on order and tidiness. Teachers are not lazy, but this is simply not their job. They should be freed to give their whole thought, in advance preparation, and during the precious minutes of the class, to the main work of teaching.

In addition to the stock materials mentioned above, if you are the kind of teacher who employs the new activity teaching, and whose plans frequently issue in creative projects, you will at times require special materials. These arise from the venture in hand, and are often improvised out of things found in the homes. The more persons who bring these, the better educationally. Most of these things are brought by special assignment —if the teacher knows his art, and does not rob his pupils of their responsibilities.

You get the general idea. The teacher always has to be aware of equipment and materials, and the best way is to anticipate, be ready, and have as much in hand in advance as possible.

One fine teacher had her own parent-teacher meeting early in the fall to plan the year's work. At a tea at her home she asked the mothers of the children in her class, "What can you do to make this year's class more interesting?" The outcome was new curtains and pictures for the classroom, several new books for the browsing table, aprons for the pasting time, and subscriptions to Church papers and a parents' magazine for the group. They agreed, best of all, to try to have one parent present to help with the class each Sunday.

5. SUPERVISION

Many a fine teacher has deteriorated because no one ever visited his class or made suggestions. As long as class work goes along, Sunday after Sunday, without any complaints from parents, the teacher soon begins to feel overconfident, that his work is good enough. Or that nobody in the Church cares, and the job can't be very important.

A teacher who had a parent visit her class was embarrassed because she had not prepared her story very well. She said afterwards that she nearly went to pieces when she noticed that the mother was taking notes. She had thoughts of being rebuked on her orthodoxy, her discipline, her Bible facts, or anything. It turned out, however, that the mother was an appreciative and kindly person who had simply wanted to know what work her child was doing.

The public schools have long recognized the value, indeed the urgent necessity, of checking up on the work of all teachers. The office of supervisor has become a recognized function, and the techniques of this official are gradually being improved. In some towns the principal is expected to visit classes and do this supervision. In the better arranged systems, a separate, skilled worker does nothing else.

The supervisor arrives at the schoolroom when a recitation is starting. She sits in the back of the room while the teacher conducts the class. The teacher may even call on the supervisor to take part. Thus the children get to know the supervisor as their friend, and as a part of the system.

The supervisor has a regular appointment, usually each week, with every teacher. Here comments are made on details of class work observed, and suggestions are offered. The teacher submits work charts for the next few days (usually the week) showing how she intends to divide her days, and the scope of each lesson. Encouragement and helpful criticisms are given.

When this system of supervision is first started in some towns, the teachers say they are nervous, over-anxious, and on the defensive. They dread the coming of the supervisor, and do not do their best teaching when she is watching. Soon, however, they learn that she is not their hostile critic, but their friend who can help them in their weak spots.

Applied to the Church School, the objective and method is the same. Somebody of ability, tact, and understanding should be expected to visit all classes regularly for this purpose. In many schools, the superintendent of the department may do it. The best reason the rector should not have any class of his own, in most small places, is that he may be free to visit and advise.

Naturally some standards must be applied, and certain tests used to improve all sides of the teaching. The following are some items in a check-list which may easily be applied on the first visit, and used in personal conferences, or at teachers' meetings afterwards.

A Supervisor's Check List

1. *Teacher's Personality:*
     Appearance_____
     Vitality, health, dynamic_____
     Attitude_____
     Manner (quiet, sincere, cheerful, not nervous, friendly?)_____
     Voice_____

2. *Teaching Skill:*

    Discipline (constructive, positive, purposeful?)——

    Materials (ready, in order, well-planned?)——

    Opening (point of contact, control of atmosphere, interest caught?)——

    Lesson (well prepared, moved smoothly, stayed on subject, arrived somewhere?)——

    Response (do pupils talk up readily, catch teacher's thought, follow guided discussion?)——

    Proportion (period well planned, does not run out of material, is finished, reaches a conclusion?)——

    Activities (planned, purposeful, natural, suitable?)——

The supervisor uses an agreed scoring method, such as 10 for perfect under each heading, down to 0 for complete failure. There are other points which might be added, if considered helpful, or as the year goes along and teacher and supervisor are forming a mutually helpful team. Thus: Does the teacher seem to be growing, acquiring new knowledge and skills? Are her records in order? Does she have any contact with the homes? Is she a thoughtful "housekeeper" of the classroom, both before and after each period? Is she asking for and securing any home work?

Whether supervision is systematic and regular, or only now and then, the honest teacher really wants to know if he is accomplishing his best. He sincerely wants to be a success, not just to be passing the time. We all need to know that someone is watching us.

But best of all, we all respond to praise. It is the quickest acting and headiest of all tonics. Many a time a teacher must have wished that somebody would drop in today—anybody— just to have an appreciative person witness his work, and perhaps have a pleasant word for him. The stimulus of earned and sincere praise is a necessity of all normal life. And here the Church School is perhaps needlessly weak, where it might so readily be strong. Few ever take the trouble to show appreciation to the teacher, or if so, they are those who mean well, but are not equipped to make any really intelligent comment. Without some official super-critic or supervisor, it must seem to the teacher that nobody really cares.

In line with the above, one might ask, "Since there is no attempt at supervision in our school, how can I get advice?" The answer is that you can ask for it. You can always ask the rector to visit your class and tell you what is wrong with it. Of course, on that Sunday you naturally get up your best lesson, and try harder than usual. But his comments, especially if in the form of a letter, written later, are sure to be helpful. Or, one can seek out some skilled public school teacher, or even a professional supervisor, with the same request. Or, at the teachers' meeting, you might bring up the subject, and propose that a scheme be set up for marking the teachers. Starting almost as a game, it might lead to regular guidance, and the whole quality of the teaching in your parish be raised.

6. LET'S GO VISITING

Few teachers ever see other teachers at work. Tips on successful methods used elsewhere, it is true, sometimes trickle in to us. But practically every teacher works in a vacuum. Whether you have taught one year or twenty, think a moment and ask yourself, "How many classes have I actually visited since I was a child?" Only a few can be recalled, and these more than likely were ineffectual and not inspiring. Indeed, just as it is unfortunately true that "preachers seldom hear sermons" (because they must all be in their own pulpits at the same hour), so it is true that teachers, being all engaged with their work at the same hour, cannot see other teachers in action.

Yet the value of visiting a good teacher is obvious, and is

widely used as a means of preparing teachers in the public institutes and teachers' colleges. Always there is required a certain number of hours of observing actual class work, followed by additional hours spent in practice teaching, under supervision. The best school systems keep their teachers at this, in order to grow and not to become stale. Many of us recall that pleasant half-day of liberty we were granted every now and then because it was "Teacher's Visiting Day." Then we children might have vaguely wondered whom our teacher visited. We cared only for the freedom, and noticed merely that our entire school building was closed. Looking back, we realize that, by arrangement of the Board of Education, neighboring schools were in session that day, and that our teacher had been required, as part of her job, to visit the room assigned of the same grade. Now and then, too, we recall, there were times when our own teacher primed us intensively for several days "to make a good impression," and then one day we had two visiting teachers who sat around and watched while we recited.

Any teacher gets into a rut, all too readily, and contact with the methods of others, by actual observation, is one of the best remedies. When the rector or superintendent finds that you, for instance, are not doing consistently good work or are not "catching on," the most immediate help and encouragement that he can give is to arrange a visit to "see how it's done in other places." This type of help can be arranged much more effectively than by offering a book to read, or than by a personal conference. The leader can remark tactfully, "You say the children don't respond. Perhaps you have run out of ideas. The teacher of our Fifth Grade, Miss Anderson, is an old hand at teaching. I always get help when I listen at her class." And so, after a little persuasion, you are induced to spend the entire period the following Sunday with Miss Anderson's class, a substitute being provided for your class that day.

When a teacher of Eighth Grade boys feels that he cannot manage them and is not getting the lesson across, he might be reminded that these same boys are sitting in the public school, in classes often four or five times as large as those at church, and for five hours a day, five days every week. Their teachers who accomplish this miracle are ordinary, intelligent people whose equipment is a certain amount of training and the know-how of experience. That know-how can be picked up. The best and simplest way is to see those teachers in action, not to hear them tell of it.

Therefore, when I think a teacher needs special improvement in his classroom procedures and fundamental devices, I tell him he ought to arrange his work so that he can drop in at the corresponding room in one of the public schools. If he does, he may see some of the same children he has on Sunday (and they will be truly delighted to see him there) obediently studying, reciting, copying, with none of the rudeness, noise or unruliness he has come to consider practically normal in his Sunday class. Then he notices just how the teacher words her requests, how she manages the distribution of supplies, moving about, reciting.

After such a visit, when a Church School teacher had taken notes for the entire afternoon session of a Sixth Grade room, the following was handed to the rector:

Some Methods I Observed

The teacher never raised her voice. The pupils seemed to listen harder when she talked very quietly. She was strict, but they seemed to like her. Only one person was allowed to talk at once. No lolling in seats. The children couldn't kick under the table, as we are arranged at church. Short periods of silent study on the text, often with a leading question on blackboard—what to be looking for. Discussion period was about something they had already studied, not about new material—not just pumping them for ideas. One bright pupil was allowed to come forward and conduct a review, phrasing the questions himself. Teacher knew her stuff, but she let them dig it out, didn't just tell them everything.

Some parishes, to make this visiting a reality, arrange a Sunday when there are no classes, but the whole school is kept together, after the opening worship, for a movie or some special speaker. The teachers have all, by arrangement, gone over to a neighboring parish, where the authorities (properly forewarned) have a little better than usual performance for the benefit of their visitors. In smaller towns, with only one parish, it has been found helpful to visit classes of special excellence (by arrangement with the pastors) in good Sunday Schools of other churches.

The best way to prepare for this visiting day is to hold a general teachers' meeting, where the method is explained, the desire aroused, and all are given outlines of points to be observed.

7. ACTIVITIES FOR BOYS

When the sexton reports that the Boy Scouts broke another table last night, some vestryman is sure to remark, "Boys are just too full of energy. We'll just have to think up some more ways to keep them busy so they can work off their steam. It's rugged work, but we must find good leaders for them." In such a summary is unconsciously stated the whole program and solution of the "boy problem" in the Church.

Many parishes approach a solution by the short cut of providing facilities such as table tennis, billiards, gyms and equipment, lockers and showers, "juke boxes," and the like. Money for them is spent in spurts, often lavishly. And then the parish fathers vainly imagine they have done their duty. But your boys and girls need very few expensive tools. A suitable place where they may work out their meetings without interference is usually enough. They will acquire what equipment they need as their enthusiasms and programs call for it. And to add each thing, by their own group thinking and co-operative work, is by far the better educational way. To have equipment handed to them often only kills initiative and interest.

We still need to study parish life to be sure that boys have plenty of experiences in and around the church and parish house. There are many duties, parts of programs, creative work which can be assigned to them for their own development, not merely to use up energy. Many a rector, deciding upon things to be done, does them himself (or asks the faithful few he has always employed), and so cheats his youngsters of the joy of sharing by doing. Almost as disastrous as this is the abrupt dumping of a task on "the boys" without first warming up their interest and motivating them. Neither way is educationally correct. In between lies the happy, broad way of intelligent leadership.

Teachers need to cultivate this ingenuity of inventing small jobs, within the unfolding of a project, and the assigning of them in such a way as to get interested and happy participation. The slogan here is, "Few things need to be done. But people need the experience of doing many things." One might add the deeper wisdom in the words, "Life is not the flame, nor the candle, but the burning."

Teachers come to know, after long years, that better than telling it is discussing it. But better than discussing it is finding out the facts for yourself. And better even than finding out the facts is doing something about it yourself. Always we get back to this: activity is the key to learning. Each pupil, in his turn and for himself, must go through the mill of experiment. There are some seeming short cuts to experience, but never any real substitute for personal activity.

Yet the traditional set-up and method of our classwork is such that we do little more than talk. Then we adjourn for another talk next Sunday. How can we introduce more activities into our system? Special assignments work well in small schools. A list of these, thought up between times, should be a real part of every teacher's preparation. Serving at the altar is the accepted practice for boys, and all should be called upon for this more often than is the case. Wise priests "work in" extra boys, as many as possible at each service, for the good of the boys.

One rector invented the office of school verger. He wears a collegiate gown, carries a home-made wooden mace. A number of older boys are given this honor in turn, by Sundays. The regular duties of the verger are typed on a heavy card, which hangs on a nail, always in the same place. The verger must arrive early, find the card, and do or check everything on it. To it are clipped the special duties which have arisen during the week. Here is a typical list:

1. See that acolytes are vested, candles lighted on time.
2. See that alms basons are in place.
3. See that every teacher's class box is in place, chairs in order (*A good check on sexton and secretary*).
4. Are pencils in boxes sharpened?
5. Are attendance charts, blackboards, etc. ready? Chalk and eraser at each?
6. Check on banners, Bibles, Prayer Books, etc.
7. Check on lesson for lay reader.
8. Secure and post a boy to manage doors (on cold days).
9. Lights all on; and off at close.

8. WORKBOOKS

A new form of pupil's book has appeared within the past few years and has enjoyed a wide sale. The poor, confused clergy will try anything. One popular course has gone all-out for the workbook form, for all ages.

Workbooks first arose in the public schools as a convenient form for notebooks, as a means of ready drill in objective information or skills. When workbooks began to appear in the Church, they were based on these already published for the public schools. A review of the ones *now* offered for sale would surprise the writers of some Church workbooks, who would learn that there have been many improvements in the method, where it has survived.

Public school workbooks cover such subjects as arithmetic, geography, history, civics, and literature. The term of late has been largely displaced by such expressive titles as "Think & Do Book," "Understanding and Practicing," "Pupil Activity Text Book," and "Objective Tests." On the whole, most public school systems have abandoned workbooks as pedagogically inadequate.

In all cases, the object is not simply to fill in the blanks and do the activity assigned. The workbook is intended to be used in the full stream of other class activities. The devices of socialized recitation, investigation, silent reading, home work, memorizing, etc., are all assumed to be used. In short, the public school workbooks are intended to be used by a teacher teaching a large subject, with several source books, and with wide teaching skill.

I confess that I have largely discarded workbooks, as at present offered to us by Church publishers, for these reasons:

(1) They make lazy teachers. A teacher may get by with

little or no preparation, and yet seem to be covering the course.

(2) They discourage the best teachers. The form of expression provided is so limited, or takes so much time, that original projects seldom arise.

(3) They are limited to a few devices: true-false, missing word, copy here.

(4) They place the emphasis on pencil activity (in which some pupils are characteristically backward), rather than on the social elements of class teaching.

(5) They are quite often not fitted to the children's vocabulary, or the answers are not clear. Then the teacher has to tell them what to write in the blank. More often, she has to look in the back of the teacher's guide! Do you call *that* teaching?

(6) They present mostly objective facts and inspire little originality or enthusiasm.

With attention, all of these may be corrected. But they reveal the trend. The basic limitation of the workbook is that it arises solely from the personal ingenuity of the author. Novel ways of stimulating the pupil to think, by devices of partial writing, have been invented by skilled teachers. These have been seized by editors and too often made tedious by being used over and over. The printed workbooks, at present, lack sparkle, diversity, and real ingenuity. Only the really very clever and ingenious person, full of his subject, and overflowing with years of happy experimental methods worked out in real teaching, should ever attempt to write a workbook.

Some new methods which are not found in the Church books include: Correct the error (cross out wrong word, and write the right one above). Sort out definitions of terms. Map with numbered locations: locate cities printed on margin by means of number. Memorizing help through novel type forms and arrangements. Pictures partially drawn, to be completed by pupil. Underscore words you do not understand. Identify sketches.

The possibilities of workbooks, properly designed, and used, should not be overlooked. Here are some good points: They provide immediate pupil activity, with the deep satisfaction of accomplishment. They may stimulate comprehension and interpretation of material. They make up for the children's slow and awful handwriting. They set a norm of achievement to which the slowest may be encouraged to attain. They hold up an ideal of good workmanship: you either finish this 100% correctly, or you don't.

A suggestion to vital teachers: make up *your own* workbook, based on your present textbook, as you go along. All you need is a typewriter, and some samples of printed workbooks for ideas. Then improve on them. But don't try to invent something for *every* lesson. And don't—please don't—rush to a publisher with your script. Let it be criticized by somebody who is not afraid to offend you, and who is an old teacher. Then let your sheets be used in real teaching by several teachers, under field conditions, for a year or more.

9. THE TEACHER'S NOTEBOOK

Most good workers are systematic. To have a good over-all system well established, ready to use, saves much strain, and releases us for better work. Things to be done repeatedly— whether in office, kitchen, or school—should be *set up* in some efficient form which will release the worker from making fresh decisions over trivial matters. With such a system carefully adopted at the start, you can approach each fresh job with pleasure, knowing that the work is already in a familiar pattern and that you can start at once without any preliminary straightening out of your equipment.

This is especially true of the teacher's management of the

materials he uses in class. Clearly he must have a notebook. But how shall it be organized?

There are certain things you must always have at hand, in the class and between times. They must be so convenient and so simply arranged that everything is at your finger tips. Five main divisions, at least, will have to be provided: the class roll of names, the new lesson, recent old lessons, future plans, and things being memorized.

If you will follow me, I'll set you up in business with an outfit that will solve at least a quarter of your troubles. First, get a looseleaf notebook which you will be proud to show. What size? The huge, full-sized ones always seem so very bulky, cannot be stowed out of sight, and are a trouble to transport back and forth. Yet if this size appeals to you, use it. The half-size is better, the three-ring kind, with pages about 5½ by 8 inches. I've known teachers who like the very tiny ones, and have hand-writing that fits them. But your notebook must suit you. You may get ruled sheets, or you may prefer the blank ones, which you can use in your typewriter.

Now, make some divider pages, of heavier material, with those grey index tabs pasted on the edges. There are to be five main divisions of your book, each labelled, in the order given below.

(1) *Pupils*. Here, just inside the cover, is your class roll, for your personal record of attendance and for all the other personal reminders referring to each child as the year goes along. No stock ruled pages are available, and your own spacing is best, anyway. You will wish every name, address and telephone, and other little points which designate each child (birthday, public school, Baptized, Confirmed, choir, Scouts, etc.). You may often want to use this list and it should be with you always —therefore in your notebook, which you take back and forth between your home and church.

This is your convenient working list. If you are a teacher who will not waste precious time in a roll-call, you will check over the attendance from memory immediately after the class period. Perhaps you will want to make some character notes about each one. There will not be room for much of this on the front page, but some teachers keep a separate list, often at home, for their own guidance through the year, of each child's characteristics. Such a list will give you room to add your private notes, from time to time, of your impressions. You think you have it all in your head, but it is good practice to jot down some of these things: health, physical traits, likes and dislikes, special problem with him, home situation, his brothers and sisters, etc. Now and then, say on a Sunday afternoon, when your class experience is still fresh in memory, you will run through this private list, and make a few jottings—how this one responded to the story, what to use to interest this child some day, a good or bad activity of another. (This special list and character notes may not appeal to all, but is mentioned here, in case it appeals to you.)

(2) *New Lesson*. Here, just behind the class roll, where you can turn to it with assurance, is your teaching outline for today's lesson. You made it out yesterday, and re-arranged the sheets so it would be right here, on the first page. This is the boiled-down result of this week's preparation, your working chart for the skilful management of the period. You have it almost engraved on your mind, but as you teach you have it open before you, just to prevent wandering. Later in the week, when you are preparing your next lesson, you will open the rings and slip this page on top of the old lesson outlines, just inside the heading Old Lessons.

(3) *Old Lessons*. Here you will want, for ready reference, some of your recent lesson outlines. But, as the year advances, this will grow too bulky, and the earlier ones should be stored

at your desk at home, where you can refer to them in preparing examinations, or for other years. But don't let your book get too fat. You don't want to lug paper every week.

(4) *Coming*. After this divider you keep a half-dozen blank pages for quick notations in class: when they voted to have a tea, to have a committee meeting. Anything that arises in class which you will want to know quickly, is swiftly jotted here. This may not be the neatest part of your notebook, but it will often be the handiest. If you make a promise, even a little one, jot it down, and be sure to look at this page when preparing. It will settle lots of arguments. It will help you remember materials: "New paste. Nat'l Geog. on Siam. Letter from M. Gold stars. 2 scissors." Here will be written any assignments, too: pupil's name and what he agreed to do or bring. Above all, jot down any long-range matters which seem shaping up in the project manner: "More information about making the panel." "Date at Orphans' Home for our visit." "Get a parent to help on exhibit."

Don't trust your memory, in the busy confusion of being "on location" with your children. Jot anything down in the "Coming" pages.

(5) *Memory Work*. Memory items are scattered all through the lessons. No matter how inadequate may be your printed texts, they call for *something* to be memorized. And since you cannot often accomplish on the set day the exact or whole item required, you can keep your materials here, for drill when convenient. Some schools and a few dioceses set up a complete year's schedule of required memory work for each grade, and if that is your case, you will wish this material ready at hand. Have all memory items typed completely in this last section of your notebook. Then you can turn to a given item—the psalm, the prayer, the portion of catechism, or whatever—at an instant's notice, and start a drill without delay.

You might allow each child to write his name on the margin of the page in your book, as a proud record (and convenient for you, too) of his achievement. Of course, your goal is to have *every* pupil learn every prescribed item, not just hit at it, by the end of the year. Your children will be interested in memorizing if you go back to it repeatedly, if only for a few moments each week.

The foregoing plan, with its five divisions, is the "standard teacher's notebook," as I have worked it out in my parishes. Sometimes it has been provided for all teachers, ready to use. But it is better—if you take a tip from the educational methods advocated throughout this book—for each teacher to decide to set up his own notebook, and then to figure out the details in his own way. The best ones will, anyway. The poor ones don't even know how to use crutches.

There are possibilities of divisions beyond these five. For example: For My Own Growth (lists of books you want to get). Pictures. Cartoons. Inspirational Clippings. Stories which Illustrate. Strong Quotations. Poems that Inspire. Christian Leaders. Wholesome Humor. Prayers. Such a scheme makes of your book almost a working file, but it will not be a burden if you feel the urge.

Personally, I think it is enough to have a mysterious back section or folder called "Reserve Ammunition." Here you may look, when, in some hard-pressed moment to hold the line of interest, you want something vital, different—and you want it *now*.

Will you consider starting a good, workable notebook now? You will be teaching for many years, you know. Each lesson period is a small front-line battle. Do you wish to advance to it barehanded, without any weapons, your gear all snarled up? Or will you be fully prepared to establish a beachhead and be ready to advance into the fray when opportunity presents itself?

10. YOUR LESSON OUTLINE

Mrs. Van, a new teacher, showed me her lesson outline for next Sunday. She laughed a little apologetically as she handed me merely a small white card on which were a few headings in her own small, clear hand. I read:

Sun. aft Epiph—Jan. 7

1. Lord's Prayer with pauses.
2. Six phrases for poster (on blackboard)
3. Hallowed: Discuss "Wonderful things."
   (Read to them: I Wonder. . . .)
4. Saying Thank You. Ps. 67:3-4; 98:4-6.
5. Grace at meals. Drill.
6. Start writing our Litany.
   (Drill on season: Epiph yesterday)

"I have the second grade," she reminded me, "and last Sunday we started on a new Christian Education Unit called *We Talk With God*. It's nice to start on an entirely different topic after Christmas."

When asked to explain further the mysterious code on her card, she told me, "It's just a final summary, to help me in class so I won't forget what I've planned to do. I make it out after I have prepared my lesson."

"You see," she went on, "the children decided last week to make posters about the Lord's Prayer. I thought we would open by saying the Prayer together, but pausing to mark the different sections. That's number one on the card. Then, right after they are seated, I plan to follow up that idea, asking how we might divide the Prayer for posters. I intend to go to the board (they write so poorly) and write the Prayer, separating it into six parts, each one to be the subject of a separate poster. We'll number them, and begin to study each for ideas that we could show in some picture or symbol. But we won't start work on the posters this Sunday.

"The rest of the outline is the same. Just enough to help me remember my plan. If I don't have it before me, we might not get anywhere before the time is up."

The only other material this teacher had was a sheet on which she had copied a poem, some verses from the psalms, and sample of a short Litany. Thus equipped, she could have her hands free, need not fumble with any books and markers, and could hold the attention of every child, every minute.

Before you come to class, you must not only have been through your lesson carefully, but must have *thought it through*, in your own mind, as a plan of action. What shall I do first? What next? When shall I introduce some activity? Your lesson, as finally enacted around the class table, will be a continuous performance in which either the teacher stage-manages well, or the pupils (demoniac possessed) run away with the show. There will be no repeat performance. This one hour (much less, in most parishes) is yours out of eternity. In this short time, impressions may be made, steps taken, and thoughts started, which may change the whole course of many lives. Theory, and fine moralizing? But it's true. *This hour is yours.*

The outlines or "session plans" provided in some published texts can never anticipate the conditions of your class, this Sunday. The editor is, in a sense, an irresponsible party, quite academic. He doesn't have to meet with *your* boys. He is far from the firing line. Such printed outlines help, if only as a start for your own plan. For one thing, you will have to reject certain items. And your own ingenuity (you have plenty of it, I hope) will always cause you to put in ideas and material from your own experience bins. After all, the editor is only a human being who has been asked, (or, in these latter days, more likely has rushed in) to write the script for the course or unit. What has become of the sincere challenge in the printed line which used to appear in the title page of all the Christian

Nurture Series, "For trial use, in the hope that the experience of teachers, through the leading of the Holy Spirit, may constantly enrich and improve the course"? The earnest teacher, in her class, is the real test-pilot for any printed text. You, too, can edit a course. Any thoughtful and sincere teacher can make up a good lesson—and should, more often than is the case.

But a little more about working outlines. The teacher who comes to the class period with no clear plan or intention only courts another failure or mediocre lesson. Either he has an outline on paper, or a memorized plan in his head. A few people, it is true, accustomed to public appearance, can so marshall their materials mentally that they know exactly what they will do, and in the performance will carry through almost exactly as planned. They have made the inward decision, "I will do this first, then tell this story, and leave time for that activity at the end."

Yet for most teachers a written outline is necessary. It is the evidence of one's preparation—a weapon ready at hand in all unforeseen surges of the class movement. It gives balance and proportion to the timing. Kept in one's notebook, it serves as a reminder for improvement, and a ready record of preceding Sundays. Your outline will be your own, in your own manner. One teacher, being eye-minded, used colored pencils and symbols to catch his eye on his outline. Here is another sample, which stresses *places* and *movement* about the class-room. (It is from Christian Nurture, 7th grade.)

Standing, silent: Pause. Then class prayer together.
Seated in circle: (a) call for reports: John........size of Sea of Gal.
    Wilbur, def. of a miracle.
  (b) Tell, "A Busy Day" [Outline on other side of card]
  (c) Discussion: What makes us well? Health. Knowledge. Why
    could our Lord heal? His power over nature (the storm.)
Go to table: Work on lantern slides.

It is clear that this teacher had discovered the advantage of a change of place and position to relieve restlessness and increase interest. Besides the usual elements, he thought out carefully the handling of his group, like a squad at drill.

Another teacher, having seen his finest efforts wasted by the time running out, planned everything to the minute. He claimed that he could stick to his schedule almost exactly. Here is one of his outlines. It is on Church History, based on Bishop Wilson's *The Divine Commission.*

9:50—Open. Discuss: What is a monk? a nun?
>A young Egyptian 250 yrs before Christ (Anthony). Discuss Anthony's decision. Have a pupil read S.Matt 19:16-23 (Rich Young Ruler).
>Is this a call for everyone? Tell story St. Martin & cloak. Story of St. Anthony and his followers.

10:05—Pass out workbooks. Study and write p. 45.
10:20—Close workbooks. Discuss life in a monastery: prayers—work—manuscripts—teaching. Then write p. 47.
10:40—Memory drill.

Notice how this teacher thought out just when to give out the workbooks, when and what to write in them, and when to close them for a time of talking. He knew, perhaps from sad experience, how having workbooks in hand can prevent effective teaching, and make class activity monotonous, with much resultant restlessness. It is the great curse of workbooks that they defeat the very objects they were invented to accomplish, and they notoriously make lazy teachers, who do little preparing. But as solid material for a variation of manual work (writing) and some self-expression, they may have their place. But that place is only now and then, and for part of a page. And never, never Sunday after Sunday.

"Must I always make an outline?" asks the new teacher. The answer might well be, "Yes, every Sunday for at least two years." After that, your experience may carry you through a studied variation of these elements: listen; discuss; make; act; write; drill—each in the right proportion and order. Outlines are best *always*, if you ask me, till death do us part. And that means a *fresh* outline, even on a familiar course—not using last year's cold card. If I catch you with the textbook in your hand, I'm almost certain you did not prepare; if you have your outline, I'm sure you did.

Possibly the greatest value of a plan, whether written or formed mentally, is that you must make up your mind—*your* mind for *your* pupils. Those precious forty minutes are the one time in a whole week, when the Church, through you, has her chance. Textbooks are increasingly suggestive, less and less worked out into the last detail. Editors more and more require that the teacher shall adapt, digest, select, condense, arrange, and invent material. In the planned presentation he must use every device which imagination, experience, ingenuity, and charm can devise. *That* is teaching!

Your outline, then, is a little script for a well prepared drama, with a limited cast, and a minimum of discordant sound-effects. Better to say, "It says here," than, "I wish you'd behave!"

11. THE FINISHING TOUCH

The last section gave some practical suggestions about making your working outline to use in class. This is on the side of teaching skill and efficiency. Yet ours is not ordinary teaching, as in the secular school classroom. This is for eternity. This is "for keeps." St. Paul, a keen student and speaker, but a better pastor, knew that knowledge shall vanish away. He had found that only the living touch of love endures.

The Church teacher is the living exponent of Christian love. Somehow, with whatever tools he is given or can contrive, he must *get through* to the heart of his pupils. And in this he does not have to work alone. But he must learn how to work with God, how to allow his Lord to stand at his shoulder. After all your ordinary preparation, you must vitalize it with your personal desire to accomplish *some spiritual impression.* Study over, outline made, boiled down, ready to pour, ask yourself, "Why am I teaching this? What will be the tone and quality of this class period?"

May I make a suggestion—rather timidly, for it is rather personal? It is this: When you are saying your night prayers on Saturday, *pray your lesson* for tomorrow to God. It is so simple, and natural.

You can pray, "Dear Father, here is our lesson, filling my mind. There is so much to it, and I'm dreadfully keen to have them respond. Is this the right way? First, we'll say the Lord's Prayer together. Then we'll talk about the posters . . . then about all the wonderful things in the world. . . . I must find *their* words to express the idea that *admiration* passes into wonder and worship. And I must have them say (not just tell them) that You made them all. I'm going to read them that verse in the textbook about 'I wonder so at many things' . . . then the points on saying Thank you . . . and the drill on grace at meals. If we have time, we'll start the new litany . . . and mention Epiphany.

"But, dear Father, keep it all simple and real. Keep me keen and alert. (Help me not to lose patience with Eddie!) And help me to love them all, for Jesus' sake. Amen."

Then a little miracle will happen, as you relax, feeling "quite good in bed, kissed, and sweet, and your prayers said" (in the words of Francis Thompson). During the night, as you sleep, God will iron out the kinks in your outline, and touch it alive through your dedicated mind. When you get to class, everything will go well. For it is His lesson, and they are His children.

V. SPECIAL PROBLEMS

1. THE BAD CHILD

At a staff meeting the teachers are comparing notes.

"This year, mine are all angels, for some reason."

"That's because that Schwartz child moved away. I had him last year, and believe me, the class was one long nightmare," said another teacher.

"Well, I'm getting Freddie tamed," adds another. "But it takes most of my attention. I make him sit right beside me, and I grab him if he moves." So speaks a determined man teacher, who has at last been touched in his pride, realizing that an eight-year-old boy has practically defeated him (a World War captain) and made him appear weak if not ridiculous.

It is such pupils who take the fun out of teaching. They also serve as barometers of our work. We might "get by" with commonplace teaching and casual preparation most of the year, giving the appearance of success with a group of quiescent children. But the troublesome child exposes us. He shows, by his extreme vitality, that we have been merely passing the time, not really teaching.

Yet, allowing for a few of the most extreme cases, *a good teacher can teach any child*. He can, because that is teaching. You are not invited to put on a performance before a prim little audience. You are given, each term, a handful of personalities. Each child is your problem, and each can be solved. There is no answer in the back of the book, but there is a solution somewhere. The finding of it may take more time, experiment, and wisdom than you are able or willing to give. This is one of the challenges of teaching.

There are several types of problem children who cause their teachers annoyance and chagrin. Each calls for a different treatment. Some cases are serious, deep rooted. Some are superficial, readily cured by a swift touch of adult purpose and direction. We can readily distinguish several types of troublesome children.

(1) *The overactive child*—Activity is the most normal characteristic of childhood, and with that we must deal all the time. But there are the few who, by temperament or native nervous constitution, seem to be always in motion. They seem to be over-stimulated, driven always by some consuming urge to do and to be, to demand and to talk, to show off, to compel attention. A few are just extremely "nervous," but many of this type probably lack self-discipline and are on the way toward becoming emotional problems later in life. As teachers, we can only be very patient with them in class, giving them activities that will hold their interest while winning their respect. At the right moments we may have to use strong discipline, starting some self-control by showing the pattern of some stronger will, and a better purpose. For these pathological children the school may have to find expert psychiatric guidance, and close cooperation with the parents.

(2) *The overnoticed child*—Some would call him simply spoiled. He has had too much attention, and has learned to enjoy it and to seek it. Not securing the notice he craves, he may work for attention in all sorts of unpleasant ways. This is often a superior child, with sensibilities misdirected. He needs activities of service, to make him aware of the needs and reactions of others, and the wholesome satisfactions of praise for worthy achievements. He needs quiet and earnest handling, to be led into feeling his place in the group life, and the deeper

joys of real achievement and well earned praise. When naughty, his case may be only accentuated by too much attention. He may need only a definite job, such as class secretary, and the experience of responsibility.

(3) *The malicious child*—You may argue that there is no such creature, that children act from impulse. But we who have taught know of cases which, at least at the moment, can only be accounted as malicious and ill willed. They may have been started off on the wrong attitude toward the teacher and the school. They may have discovered, early in their times at Sunday School, the fun of doing tricks and plaguing the adult leaders, until they were definitely in a position of active enemies of the administration.

Now and then we find a child who does unpleasant things, and we know these call for swift and decisive measures. Usually he has enough intelligence to respond wholesomely to just punishment. Yet the better way, it must be admitted, is to win his good will and co-operation. And that, brethren, takes real leadership, time, and love. Miss Morton said, "I'm going to get that boy *on my side*, and then I'll have a marvelous class!" And she did, within two months.

(4) *The overbright child*—Let the interest lag, let the simple lesson run out, and your bright child becomes the troublemaker. He has done the writing, copied the prayer, filled in the blanks, or pasted the picture. "What'll I do now?" He provides the answer by getting into mischief. To balance the tempo of your class movement between these super minds and the dullest is a feat often taxing the skill, patience, and zeal of a veteran.

In all the foregoing, the rule is: Work at difficult cases *outside of class*. Make your special plans; anticipate the troublesome, individual misconduct. "If he starts it this Sunday, I'll send him straight to the superintendent, and he will be prepared to spend some time with him." Above all, work with the parents, who are truly eager to have their children turn out well, or at least to make a good impression. A frequent talk with a mother over the phone is a great comfort, and produces surprising results.

In any event, work for a solution; do not allow the misconduct to continue, undermining the tone of your class, and wasting all your nervous force. The bad child may have to be removed from the class, by being given some invented task or sphere of activity, in order to save everything. But he is *your problem*, and if, by now, you are the teacher I think you are, you will solve it—or him.

2. THE PERSONAL CONFERENCE

A new word that has burst upon the educational horizon is *guidance*. Returning servicemen are to have guidance. Students are to be studied as cases, and given guidance. The method employed is largely the device of the personal interview in which the adviser and the student or veteran go through a prescribed routine, and notes are taken for the file.

The weak point in the scheme is apt to be the person of the leader, who is entrusted with the delicate task of drawing out the other, and presumably helping him make some constructive decisions. He is supposed to provide information, wisdom, and inspiration. Whether the system will work only time can tell. But certainly individuals need personal attention, whether mechanized or informal, and it is now recognized that teachers should provide this for their pupils.

This may well be the special rôle of the consecrated and mature Church teacher. He knows his sheep, and they know him. The week-by-week companionship of the class circle has paved the way for intimate moments of talk. At moments both unexpected and planned, the teacher has opportunity to enter into the special personal problems of his little group.

We have had a large emphasis on the class. We have prepared for the lesson, we calculate the timing of the class-period, the group activity, the project arising from the common mind, and completed by joint efforts.

Many a teacher will arrive just in time for the class, and dash away immediately after its close. All this has tended to make teachers forget that all the time they are dealing with lone individuals. The group method of teaching is an economy, and in some ways a necessity for teaching. But all the time it is Tommy and Helen and Wilbur and Carolyn who go back to their own homes, and whose growing character is our real problem.

Consider the special opportunity of the Church teacher. The public school teacher has thirty to fifty, while he has only ten or a dozen. The former cannot follow up individuals. But the Church teacher can single out his children for special moments, can deal with their personal needs as they arise.

A good way is to start taking notes about your pupils. Some day, when preparing your lesson, try composing a character sketch of each child. Just attempting this you will begin to realize how dimly and how impersonally you have perceived the personalities of many of them. You start to jot down: "Milton—rather nervous, very poor writer, never can unfasten own overshoes. I can't seem to win his affection. Never scuffles with the other boys. Is the quickest to find places in Bible. Has a stamp collection. Only child. His mother overconcerned about his health."

You knew this already, and much more. But the writing of it down helps you clarify and often to see an underlying problem that you would miss in the swift movement of the class period. Moreover, your rough notes, reviewed now and then, help you to plan and build for that child. You realize you must take the trouble to talk about that point, to get his confidence.

And that means some moments found apart with him, no matter how arranged. One method for taking notes is to have a rough outline to fill in for such areas as these: Physical, nervous, social conduct, skills, needs help in ———, home situation, special interests, dislikes, achievements.

Some of these special moments come unplanned. You arrive at church early, and there is your boy. In a short, direct talk you try to get across your special point for him. It may be something which calls for a special interpretation. But most guidance must be done by the sought out personal interview. Then, in a leisurely talk, without interruptions, you can start ideas, and develop attitudes. It isn't easy. Only love and practice and patience will begin to get results.

I recall a woman who did a unique work of personal guidance through a junior altar guild. The plan was simply for a girl to meet with her and sew on altar things. As they sewed they talked. Though seemingly casual, the themes were things that mattered. "I learned more from Mrs. Atterby than in any class I can remember," a young woman told me in after years.

"Teaching is guidance" is the new slogan. Groping lives must be helped to find their own right way. There are adjustments to community life to be made, home handicaps to be overcome, personality patterns to be untangled. No two are alike—the fat, the skinny, the homely, the frail. There is self-consciousness, timidity, quick anger, defeatism, vanity, showing off, compensations of all sorts.

Personality persists, yet may be slowly modified. Hence the need for your notes, and your prayers, your planning and persistence. If you would think of the class period as only the beginning, of personal contacts as the real opportunity, you would have a new conception of your work. The rector has assigned you these few sheep of the flock, not for a crowded hour on Sunday morning, but all through the year. It is your deep joy to lead them. You are accountable to the Shepherd of them all, who gave His life for each.

3. CONSTRUCTIVE DISCIPLINE

"Isn't Mr. Winter's class terrible!" Everybody in the school is saying it. Just when classes were going nicely last Sunday, there was a crash and shrieks of laughter from the alcove. A boy, who had been balancing on the back legs of his chair, had at last fallen backwards. The superintendent, ever vigilant as an officer for maintaining quiet, had rushed in, to find Mr. Winter apologetically trying to stop the confusion and hearty laughter. He was trying to smooth it over, to get them back into reasonable quiet again.

He had never thought to punish the boy, nor to check him when he first began to teeter in his chair. It was, to him, just one of many forms of boyish restlessness, which he frankly does not know how to manage.

It is true that poor Mr. Winter doesn't have much chance with the makeshift arrangements in the parish house. There is a screen in front of the alcove he must use for his circle of fifteen small boys. He has no table for them to work at, only a small blackboard, which sometimes falls down. He knows that five other adjoining classes can hear his class, and have complained frequently. This makes Mr. Winter terribly self-conscious. He is more concerned now with keeping them quiet than anything else. He will bribe, promise, cajole. He lives in a momentary dread of a fresh outburst of a shout, a laugh, or a crash. Although he labors to prepare his lessons, he just doesn't seem to be able to get "good discipline." Yet the teachers within earshot have little trouble in maintaining order, and in conducting peaceful and attentive classes. Why?

We must analyze Mr. Winter for a bit. He actually expects bad order. He counts on it, dreads it, but does not know how to head it off. It is true he does not desire it. But he has long had so much noise that he is content if he can now get through the period without too much clamour. He is desperate, but resigned. Frankly he has no picture of the good order he really wishes. He has no plans for real discussion, knows few devices for activity.

He does not check the first outbreak of disorder. Several voices join in the talk, the pitch of the teacher is raised to be heard, and almost in a moment all are talking loudly. (This is the normal noise-hunger of growing children, which flares up instantly at the slightest suggestion. They like noise.) Instead, he must learn to demand, every time there is a violation, "Only one person talks at a time in our class!"

If I were Mr. Winter, I think I would spend one whole Sunday session straightening out the class attitude. The approach would be the club idea, that we might organize, with officers, and rules. We would elect the usual four officers, and then would come the question, How can we improve our class? Soon, there would be one boy at the blackboard putting down things we all agreed to. With very little suggestion they would soon have some things like the following agreed upon:

Class Rules

1. Not to chew gum.
2. Not to kick each other.
3. Not to tip back in your chair.
4. If tardy, come in quietly, and explain to class why you are late.
5. Bring your book.
6. Do not talk without permission.
7. Only one person talks at a time. Do not interupt.
8. Do something every Sunday to help the school.

So the list is accepted, and the class starts out with a new character, formulated by the boys themselves. The teacher will see that the list is kept posted, and enforced. If violated, the class may be appealed to to decide the punishment. Everything is done to make the group conscious of itself as a group, not just a mob of individuals, and which has a mind and purpose and tradition of its own. Soon they will readily accept such affirmations as, "Our class is always helpful."

The last rule has in it all sorts of possibilities. It includes things like ushering, helping younger children with coats, picking up books, or whatever needs to be done. It leads to their realizing that the other classes are quiet to help *them*, and they will play the game, too.

With a fresh start thus made, Mr. Winter would be ready for some fine Sundays, provided he immediately learns some of the devices of planning activity. He will by now begin to realize that the good conduct of a class is the result of good teaching. Teachers who know their lessons, and know how to teach, confidently yet easily, have no disciplinary problems. The very word "discipline," indeed, has in it the idea of constructive teaching. It meant, and still means, "discipleship." The children are the teacher's disciples. That changes everything. They have been called—here they are, the leader's faithful dozen, separated from the world for the moment, ready and willing to do anything suggested. And Mr. Winter only tries to keep them from making too much noise! The good teacher rises to the opportunity, is inspired, works, prays, struggles, and wins.

Constructive discipleship, in which the teacher accepts his rôle of personal worker for our Lord, begins with the intense resolve not to fail, and continues in the weekly effort to get definite response and results. The teacher who has "good discipline" has a plan, and finds methods. Instead of having to stifle childhood vitality, he knows how to use it. Talk there must be, but always skilfully planned for just this age, this group. And always the talk is only preliminary to action.

Think of the many kinds of activity which may be managed, even under the inadequate conditions of the average parish. The following list will help to illustrate the things you may call upon, and should, for variety of interest:

Directed talk: Discussion, debates, reports, recitation, choral reading, Bible reading, quiz tests, reviews, memory drill.

Handwork can be used, provided it is planned for the conditions of Sunday space and time, and related to the teaching unit: Art work, not too pretentious. Crayoning, lantern slides, posters, manuscript writing, scrap books, clay modeling, flannelgraphs, sandtable.

Movement for such things as a game, contest, drill, or dramatization.

Writing, if for a real purpose, not just to fill in blanks in an editor's scheme, and of course not too difficult nor too long.

Trips or pilgrimages into the church for study of some special matters, such as the altar, font, or the vestments.

Outcomes of projects started in class: packing the box, decorating for a party, painting chairs, delivering baskets, selling things, visiting an orphanage, etc. These things, although done on a weekday, react on next Sunday's joyous class feeling.

Worship is a real activity, and may be injected into any period.

The activity method is possibly the best short way to happy teaching. It may be overdone, to the detriment of teaching the content of the lesson. But there is far greater danger that classes degenerate into mere talk, and that mostly by the teacher, with restlessness and boredom the inevitable sensation of the children. Fix your mind on this, as you prepare your lesson: What shall I have them do, what shall I start them wanting to do, in this period, or as a result of it? The truth is, Mr. Winter doesn't know what he wants. He expects nothing but "youthful energy," and knows none of the ready ways of directing it. He may be beyond repair. Yet, if he can only have a few Sundays of happy, purposeful activity, and a feeling of class unity, he will begin to learn. He will repeat his successes, and will grow in his methods and his achievements. From being a failure, on the way out, he will have become a success, on the way up. It will change his whole outlook, perhaps his whole life. He will begin to brag about his class, tell others of the stunts he has invented.

He will have met his problem, won through to the good will and following of his pupils. *That* is teaching. How can we get Mr. Winter started on the use of activities in teaching?

4. BUILDING A CURRICULUM

"My pupils don't like this course," a teacher tells me, and I know she is only covering up the fact that she can't teach the course. It is natural to blame someone else. And yet we can't blame the teacher entirely, for we have all found that certain courses are difficult to present, or weak at some points. Most often, the method and outlook of the text do not chime with the attitude and training of the teacher. It is just the wrong course for her.

No printed lessons are perfect, it is true, because they are the efforts of a writer or a board to organize materials and techniques which must, in real use, pass through the personality of each teacher, and to the personalities of real children. These are of all sorts, and largely incalculable. You never can be sure how anybody will act in response to the ideas and plans of others.

When a teacher, really trying, cannot put over the materials which have been given to him for the year, it is reasonable to ask what can be done about it. To waste a whole year in futility, annoyance, and with a diminishing class seems needless. Yet to switch to some other text is surely no guarantee of correcting the trouble. All courses have some flaws, and there is no course so perfect that it relieves the teacher from patient effort, ingenuity, and adaption.

The clergy, who have the responsibility for the success of their schools, are notoriously weak in this solution. They will try any new course offered, with only the most casual examination, always hoping that this is at last the perfect system, which they have only to order, hand out, and forget about for a year That so many of them do just this may explain so many weak schools and poorly taught children.

For the present, we must work along this line: We must teach our children, week by week. And we must work with the materials at hand, until something better appears. But the real trouble, all through, lies in the assumption in the minds of both clergy and teachers that the printed material is the most important thing. Yet if we will consider, for a moment, the whole problem of curriculum, we may get a new approach. Broadly, the curriculum is the whole plan for teaching—what to teach and when to teach it. A committee undertakes to answer the large question, "What shall we teach our pupils from the first years they can understand to the end of their school days—from about four years to twenty?" The usual way is for the committee to start making a list of yearly topics.

What shall we teach in kindergarten? What in the fourth grade? To sophomores? The result, after several sessions of the committee, is a neat list of topics, sometimes obscured by romantic titles, for each year's main objective. It is sometimes discovered that this was all done, back in the 1890's, in the

Standard Curriculum, which is still the norm if we assume the topical or content approach.

Next, each year's theme is farmed out to a likely writer or group of experts, and they eventually produce a textbook to be used as the material for teaching about thirty lessons. Now it comes to the class teacher. In effect he is told, "Your subject for the year, for these children, is the Ten Commandments, or the life of Christ, or whatever the curriculum calls for. Here is the printed book to use. Make the most of it. Have a good year."

If every teacher would look upon this ceremony of receiving the book each year as the acceptance of his marching orders, and would then try to adapt them to his own skills, and the fluid response of his pupils, we would have better teaching. To every teacher, then, the rector says, "Stick to this subject all year, as much as you can. There are other books you will need. Some of the suggestions will work, some won't. But you are the teacher, not a mechanic watching an automatic loom. This is a memorandum, not a blueprint. See that your children memorize some information, practice some worship and service, and live with you together for a year as Christian friends."

Content and method meet in the person of the teacher. He must digest the content, the substance of the Christian tradition, and then find devices by which his pupils will, as inheritors of that tradition, make it their own. No curriculum can do this for him, or them.

5. INTERRUPTIONS IN CLASS

Every teacher, old or new, at some time or other has been distressed by interruptions in the class work. This may be felt to be especially annoying when one has prepared particularly well and its eager to put over some special line of thought or project. You have your outline, your plan. You start out perfectly, and the class responds about as expected. All is going splendidly, when—bang! some word is spoken, or an accident happens, or a wrong note is struck, and the whole class period seems to have been destroyed.

You may be the intense, eager type, one of those who want things to happen just right, and truly desire results. To you such sudden breaks in the class attention come with especial annoyance and may for you spoil the whole period. They may cause you to feel frustration and despair, to say, "What's the use of trying?"

Some of the interruptions are purely external, from outside the class. The worst is the secretary (or his youthful assistant) who barges in without apology and in the middle of some hard-won attention demands a count (or a recount), or envelopes, or whatever. The children don't mind. They rather enjoy the intrusion, for it may call for some activity on their part. But, although the intruder is gone in a moment, the thread of attention is snarled. You have to recreate the tone and common thought of your group. And you are not in as good a frame of mind to do it, being now a little strained and exasperated.

Then there are those many sounds which fill a parish house or church basement at Church School time. A fraction of one percent of our parishes have separate and sound proof class rooms—the rest camp all over the premises. Some of these sounds may be dimmed by the devices of portable partitions, curtains, and other "temporary" arrangements. But for the most part they remain as a distracting background. At any moment there may be a sudden burst of laughter from a distant class, the crash of some falling chair, or even a paper dart sailing over the partition from some teacherless or unmanageable class.

In addition, there are visitors, well-meaning and usually

worth having, if only as an excuse for displaying drill. But any one, and all together, they represent those strains on the teacher's nerves which must be withstood. The solution? For each immediate case, *fight through immediately* to your former attention, keeping your calm and good nature as well as you can. For the large problem of space and rooms, stop grumbling and *kick*—often, and to the right people.

But the real problems come from your pupils themselves. A pupil arrives late. In the midst of a sentence you may have to stop and administer discipline. Or, a question is asked that seems to call for an immediate answer. For instance, you have been developing the thought of being a good soldier of Christ. You are getting along swimmingly: soldiers must be trained, endure hardships, be obedient, respect their leaders, etc. And then, Judith, who is a "deep one," remarks, "If we had peace we wouldn't have any more soldiers, would we?" You had been wondering a little about that yourself, and now you grasp at the question, developing the thought. It is one of those lucky breaks that give you a special opportunity for teaching not in the text book, but often far more valuable.

But the worst intrusion is the remark, arising from the mysterious ramifications of the child mind, which has nothing to do with the subject. Suddenly, with no connection, David says, "We're going to get our new car tomorrow." The others chime in about their cars, and you have to wangle attention back onto the main track again. Evidently you had been talking to a wandering mind.

The solution? The same for all problems of human leadership: be your best self always—adaptable, ingenious, alert, patient. Part of your preparation may be to anticipate this. ("If they start to get away, I'll switch to this story.") But always, know your main goal, and stick to your main planned procedure.

Remember this: If children's minds wander, it is largely the teacher's fault. Therefore, be alert, be prepared. The more material you have on tap, the more ammunition you have for the emergency. Above all, keep your poise, your temper. Other teachers are doing it, and so can you. These annoyances are only part of the general problem of dealing with living people.

6. CHECKING FOR RESULTS

Some teachers never seem to be interested in rounding out the year's study. They have developed the attitude of the school being a Sunday-by-Sunday matter. As long as they are there, have a lesson, or provide a substitute, they have done their duty. Now, in late Spring, the school year is running out, and they are secretly a little relieved that it will "soon be over." They have stuck to the end, to be sure, and are to be accounted faithful teachers.

But what about the year's work as a whole? You were given the year's topic: Life of Christ, the Commandments, Prayer Book, Virtues, House of God, or whatever. You received your textbook and other aids "way back there in September." Ever since, you have been trudging ahead, a lesson each Sunday. Now, it is about time each teacher began to do some checking up, both on himself and on his pupils. The sincere teacher really wants to know if he has accomplished anything. All schools have some form of final examinations, toward which much of the teaching and drill is pointed.

If there is no final test required by the school, the thorough teacher may desire now, the remaining Sundays, to round out the work by some thoughtful reviewing and drill of his own. Just to ask questions about past lessons, skimming through the book casually, is only to create boredom and little result.

You would hate to think (even though nobody else discovered it) that you had wasted your own time and your pupils' for a whole year. You will admit to yourself that they remember terribly little from week to week, and almost nothing from last fall. Just how much they know or don't would surprise you—it really would! In starting to test your pupils' knowledge, first plan the areas you wish to explore. There will be three, and each will call for different ways of testing.

(1) *General ideas, attitudes, and motives*—For this, you will think out carefully some questions, mostly in the form of imaginary problems in human conduct, hoping for response from individuals. Thus: "A boy runs noisily through the church. If you were there, what could you do about it?" "Is it possible to love the Germans?" "Why is teasing mean?" "If God made us, and everything we have, what should we do about it?" These questions should arise from topics earlier in the course and be aimed to start going the process of recollection. This will go best as an informal discussion. For older ages a short written examination on such points will require each pupil to make up his own mind and express himself in words.

(2) *Facts*—The student who says, "I never could remember dates," is typical of the thousands who look upon schooling as the quantitative lodging of facts in human skulls, ready for instant use ever after. This common resistance of some minds to definite learning of facts has to be gotten around—by steady drill and persistence, if necessary; by the contagion of enthusiasm thrown around the theme in general; and much humanizing and vitalizing of the course, if possible.

For every year's course there are certain essential facts that can now, in the closing Sundays, be drilled. Here is a call for games and contests to make it fun. The real hazard is the teacher: he must see the importance, and work at it in his lesson preparation. If his lessons have been well prepared through the rest of the year, this will now come easily. If not, he will have to wrestle with the front pages of his text, and spend some extra time on these Spring Saturdays, or else let the whole matter go by default. Therefore, go through your book and list a score or more of facts that should be known names, definitions, terms, locations, numbers, dates, characteristics. Spend some time on this list each Sunday from now on.

(3) *Skills*—Can the children find places in Prayer Book, Bible, or whatever the theme? Do they say their morning prayers? Make the sign of the cross? Pray on entering church? These may be matters of general discussion earlier, but now the teacher wants to know if every child has added these accomplishments, and may well have personal interviews, with an informal checklist to make sure. Above all, does *each child* actually know all the prescribed memory work for the year?

The closing Sundays in the Spring are your great opportunity to make up for a weak year, or to round out brilliantly a good year. Partly, you are testing yourself as you test your children. But you are mostly clinching the nails you drove in other lessons. The total impression of the year, and how its work shall linger in the lives of your pupils, depends a lot on how you manage these closing sessions.

7. WORKING FOR ATTENDANCE

A visiting speaker at a parish supper complimented the local rector on the large turn-out. "You evidently have, Sir, a most loyal and interested parish." The rector smiled gracefully, for he knew his people did care, on the whole. But he realized that this large gathering was no accident, but the result of hours of telephoning and a skilfully built-up barrage of postcards, announcements, and newspaper items. It had been hard work for several people.

Attendance must be worked for, and is worth working for. People will ultimately do what is expected of them, but in a world of many vivid appeals the Church must make its own call strong and clear. There is general publicity, but we can never relax the need for personal reminders. There comes to mind the teacher of a young men's Bible class who wrote a personal note to every one of the members every week, until the class reached nearly 200.

To secure regular attendance, the parish school in general can give certain helps. There are the varied attendance contests, which bring up group competition and make much of the fun of all being there. The individual is reached with the appeal that he is important, if only to make up the total. There has been much discussion of attendance devices and some of the following are conclusions from experience.

Systems which use pins and badges, on an increasing scale, are not only expensive, but commit the school to a year-after-year, unchanging method. If they got the results desired, they might be justified, but they tend to stimulate 100% attendance, over a long period, for a relatively few pupils—and these usually the ones who would attend regularly without any scheme, anyway.

A contest is often called for when there has been a noted slump in attendance, or an increase in tardiness. Then a short term contest will often revive good habits, and its effects last long after.

Such contests should be designed to bring out the special points that need strengthening in the school's habits. Thus, if many teachers are irregular or often tardy, allow a heavy score for the teacher's record. His non-performance will bring down the class total, and the children will attend to the rest. Perhaps you wish to stress better attendance at Church, or home-work done, or the like. Then allow more points for these.

Class contests, apart from the rest of the school, are often helpful. The unit for these is the month, or perhaps the quarter. Supply houses provide pictures with 13 stickers for a quarter. Better always, design your own scheme and chart, and let the children have a hand in making and developing it.

Tardiness is something that is like a slowly advancing disease, which paralyzes first individuals, then the whole group. It must be dealt with firmly and promptly. A good secretary does more than merely record and make curves of attendance. He will try to telephone the home of every missing child, before the school is over, or at least not later than Monday. Sickness is thus often discovered, and the clergy will know what to do. Realizing that the school is definite and expects good and prompt attendance, parents will co-operate. It is flattering to be missed.

But the broader truth must also be appreciated: attendance is the *result* of interest engendered by a vital and stimulating school and teacher. Children just can't stay away from something that is always delightful.

The best device I ever knew to break up chronic tardiness was invented by the teacher who had a fascinating serial story for the opening moments of every period. She started exactly on time, and if any child arrived late she stopped abruptly for that day. The class, thus cheated in mid-story, saw to it that the late one was on time next week.

In all this, no matter what the school does, the teacher is still the determining factor: winning individual loyalties, watching every detail, breaking up trends toward carelessness, talking to parents, using cards, notes, charts, contests. All these are in his bag of tricks if necessary.

A woman had the wrong attitude who told her priest, when

accepting her position as teacher, "I'll be there every Sunday, but don't expect me to get them out. I'll teach them, but I won't chase after them."

To her the rector wisely replied, "But that's your first problem. Attendance is the *mark* given your teaching—100% present regularly means you are an A teacher; an average of 75% present grades you as about a C. If you can't win them and keep them coming, by some means, you are not a success."

Faithful performance is a habit that grows on people with steady practice. It becomes part of their characters. But the institution calls it forth by its own definite character. A school that always starts several minutes late, that never looks up missing children, inevitably gets a ragged response. *Expect* regular and punctual attendance, note every failure, and you will get results. And in this all, every single devoted and loyal teacher is an unfailing example and a center of constructive enthusiasm.

8. STIMULATING ORIGINAL WORK

On a screen near the door of the church was a display of children's work, and several parents stopped and examined it with interest. The poster over it read, "Original Work by Sixth Grade Pupils in a Unit on Our Bible." There was a wide diversity. There were posters, scrolls like ancient Bibles, poems, illuminated manuscripts, book binding, prayers, and scrap books. Much of this, no doubt, had been stimulated by the skilful teachers of this group, but the display also revealed the undeveloped abilities of average children.

There is a persistent impression held by many parents and some teachers that original work is very rare and comes only from the child who is superior or a genius. Such work, they

say, comes from some hidden urge which they do not understand, and surely cannot start. It's just *there*—"Helen is always
doing those things"—and there's nothing we can do. Such
special performances are acclaimed and exhibited with amazement if not reverence, and are generally held to be so excep-
tional as to prove the rule. It is simply assumed that most pupils
only follow the lesson exactly, do what is expected of them,
and nothing more. The one who has done something original
is looked upon with interest, but no hope is entertained that
more pupils may be led to do creative work.

Teachers need a better point of view on this, and to have
higher hopes of response. Indeed, it should be appreciated that
if you get *any* response to your teaching, it will be original.
That is to say, unless you actually dictate the sentences to be
written, each pupil will do his part in his own way. This does
not mean always brilliant results or showy, but original—the
child's own expression, his personal and peculiar response to
the lesson. Since most of our Church School teaching is tragi-
cally limited to talk by the teacher, with more talk expected in
reply from the children, we do not often detect originality.
Yet almost every week teachers report some unexpected reaction, searching question, or quotable remark.

Here is our teaching challenge: Everyone needs the developing experience of creative work. Once, after putting a penny
into a "Your-weight-and-your-fate" machine, I received a card
which said, "165 lbs. There is something within you which is
yearning for expression. To bring it to light will be the
supreme joy of your life." My weight was wrong, but the
fortune was absolutely correct, not only for me, but for anyone
who might have drawn that card. The mere stating of it made
me resolve to get out my paint box, or write a poem—or something!

Some people early become expressive, are self-starters, and all their lives they become noted for the things they do and say. But thousands of others could have this experience, and their lives would be vastly enhanced and made happier if, somehow, they might be launched into some original work. We owe it to our children to try to help them find these hidden springs, to have, early in life, the exhilarating experience of creative achievement—to have felt, or said, "I did it myself!" And thereafter to feel confidently, "I can do things, again and again." Teachers, ordinary teachers, can bring out such moments far more often than they realize. And merely to have seen such a response come, as a result of one's teaching, is a thrilling thing. The teacher can say, "I did it!" And there comes a sense of power—"I can do it again."

A writer has suggested that there are at least four basic experiences which every person should have in order to have lived a full rounded life. These are, plant a tree, write a book, have a son, and build a house. If applied broadly and expanded into their widest meaning, these four might readily be proposed as the perfect quadrilateral of ideal experiences. To plant a tree would include any labor with nature whereby one secured returns in directed growth and harvest. The book could be any personal artistic expression, in writing, music, or the plastic arts. Instead of a son, some will have to find the experience of parenthood through teaching other folks' children, as a functioning god-parent, or as an uncle or other discerning relative. To build a house means just that, plus the deeper meanings of founding a home, and building it into a perfect thing, a corporate work of material and human engineering.

All four will be seen to arise from primitive impulses and to yield life's deepest satisfactions. It is good for a man to have done all these, nay it is necessary. You have missed part of your life if you crawl into your grave without having done the equivalent of these four.

But there is a fifth, which runs all through the others, and demands its expression at every turn. *We must find God.* To lead our boys and girls to seek and to find Him, each for himself, is the inner work of the Church teacher. Sometimes we can work, for a brief while, directly at the religious experience. More often we can only stimulate it through the other channels of life. But personal response we must work for.

Teachers can get original work more often than they do if they will come to expect it, and make room for it. Suggestion and encouragement create an atmosphere in which timid souls reach out experimentally. To suggest what others have done, to show examples, and to provide opportunity and time for individual work are essential requirements. In the rushed conditions of our usual Sunday morning this is difficult. Therefore we may have to have extra meetings of the class for activity. Original writing is not often done amidst the confusion of the class period, but suggestions made there will often induce work to be done at home. Certainly every child should not be expected to do exactly the same task, make the same article by the same pattern.

You will feel some day amply repaid for your work when a child hands you his own prayer or poem or article made. Indirectly that will be your creation, the result of your sensitive manipulation of the raw materials of child life. And it will give a joy, let me assure you, akin to the joy of God the Creator.

For if we may read the first page of the Bible with insight, we may see God, at the end of each day's mighty work, stepping back from His canvas and saying, "Not bad! . . . That's *good!*" If the great Artist can so rejoice, so does every human creature, made in that same divine image, take pleasure in the work of his own hands. To give our children—all of them—this exhilarating experience, is the happy work of the teacher.

9. THE CHRISTIAN VOCABULARY

The story of the child who complained that she could not see the "horse on the line" when the teacher had been explaining a *horizontal line* is doubtless no invention. So, too, must be the one of the child who said that the equator was "a menagery lion running around the earth." The child's meager experience makes it inevitable that he should miss the meaning of many new words, unless they are carefully presented to him at first.

The Church is not perverse nor antiquated in having a special vocabulary, because the ideas and experiences with which she deals are in a different order from those of the secular world. It is true that the early Church literally had no specialized vocabulary, but used the nearest word in the current language. Thus, elder, overseer, diocese, deacon, and others were understood in the meaning of their day. But many such words soon took on a specialized and limited meaning as certain Christian ideas were appreciated and had to be labelled and more closely defined in Church life.

One of the worst forms of "verbalizing" so much attacked today, is the inclination of some teachers to drill on the definitions of certain key words, believing thereby to equip the pupil with an experience of the ideas they stand for. Thus, the Catechism demands that we shall explain what we "mean by this word sacrament." And puts into our mouths a ponderous definition containing at least six words unknown or seldom used by twelve-year-olds.

The proper order is clearly to start with the idea, in simple language, and by illustrations easily grasped. Then the word is given, and used in conversation and sentence-making as the correct and convenient handle for the idea. Thus, the imaginative teacher tells of services in which God does special things for us. Several of these are demonstrated, visited, and in several ways experienced. Then the teacher speaks of one of these as being a sacrament. The children are asked to use the new word in sentences. Then, having acquaintance with the word, it is enriched by other associations which are gradually added by the teacher—"outwardly and visibly," "by Christ," "a means of grace," "a promise" (pledge).

Consider the fearfully technical words which we hope our people will some day understand and use accurately: Regeneration, sanctification, salvation, justification, contrition, satisfaction. Or even the apparently simpler words grace, intercession, hallow, trespasses. If we would not worry about giving our scholars these words, but would contrive to lead them to the experiences for which each stands, we might then, at an appropriate moment, provide the word.

Children do not understand many things the teacher says because of several factors, all of which the alert teacher can avoid with thoughtful planning. First, a new word, when it is introduced, should be spoken very clearly and distinctly, and in a context which gives it meaning. Thus: "Baptism is the first *sacrament* we do." (Note the simple verb.)

Second, without pausing to lodge the new word, or expound its inner meaning, pass on to teaching the meaning of Baptism, and then, when the word sacrament comes up again, take time to enlarge on its meaning and use.

Finally, be sure to come back to the new word, and allow its use by the pupils, in their own expressions (not set in a long, required formula) in several subsequent lessons and through the year. We must remember that new ideas etch themselves into our minds slowly. That takes time. But they also have to become ours by our own recall and use, until they become our own working tools. Children love word drills, if conducted with skill. "Who will make a sentence using the word grace?"

The primary years—the early grades—are especially the time

for the rapid growth of vocabulary, because experiences are being had which are novel, and which the child is eager to appreciate. His natural curiosity leads him to appropriate new words, not to show off, but as part of his reaching out for life. The teacher should not avoid words with which the child is unfamiliar, but should take care that the words are presented without misunderstanding, and are used frequently and accurately. The length of the word is no difficulty, if thus presented intelligently. But it must be a word for an idea already partially known.

We must be everlastingly alert to the real vocabularies of our pupils. Studies of public school word-lists for each grade will help. For the Church, there is a grave need for some official word lists—the words which should be known and used at each age level. Thus, when should we introduce the words *angel, inspiration, temptation, responsibility, sin, everlasting, creation, catholic, historic, conversion,* and the many other words used in religion?

A word-book is a splendid activity for a class whose teacher is alert about teaching the right use of new words. Early in the term a large blank notebook is secured and labelled and is to be kept in view at all times. When a new word is spoken by anyone, teacher or pupil, anybody may raise his hand and ask that the word be placed in the word-book. The word is placed at the top of a fresh page, often without further comment at the time. Before or after class any child may write in the book below each word a sentence using the word. Some will bring pictures to paste under words such as, *altar, chalice, surplice,* etc. Others may wish to make a sketch on the page illustrating the words such as *genuflect, crucifix, procession, lectern.* The book grows in interest through the year, and the new words become familiar friends of all.

To be certain you are not using words beyond the understanding of your children, the next time you have prepared your lesson, run through your notes and see if you can detect any words you are to use which are doubtful for that age. You may need some advice, perhaps from a critic invited to hear your teaching. But in any case be alert about your language. It is possible that your words are not touching the minds of your pupils. And if your minds do not meet, there is not apt to be much teaching.

10. INTEREST OR ATTENTION?

A returned soldier, now teaching a class of fourth-grade boys, reported the following experiment. He said, "After a few Sundays I was desperate. Finally I gave up trying to teach the lesson and asked, 'Well, what are you interested in, anyway?'

"I discovered that most of them were in a kind of neighborhood gang that played afternoons in a wooded tract and were constantly engaged in a variety of war games. They had started it during the war when they were much smaller, and it had remained a pastime.

" 'Next Sunday,' I told them, 'if you will sit very still while I teach you the lesson, I will stop ten minutes early to tell you the best war story I know.'

"I wish you could have seen the class next Sunday! Not a sound from them as I told of the attack on a German position and of the advance of our unit. This has worked so well that I do it every Sunday now. Finding intimate war stories is often hard, although I manage to invent or recall enough. But it is not nearly so hard as keeping the class from disturbing others."

Would other teachers care to comment on the following points? Did this teacher have an ideal class—"not a sound from them?" Was this good teaching—a lesson to silent pupils? How long would you expect this scheme to work? What else could the teacher have done?

Far from being a single case, the above device is adopted in desperation far more frequently than you would suppose. The common form is for the teacher to promise to read from some interesting book, "if you are good and get through our lesson first." The book may be anything—from tales of Robin Hood to selections from the *Book of Knowledge*. Now and then a teacher, with an eye for the classics, will try *Pilgrim's Progress*, but I have never known one to finish it.

The motive of such teachers is not wrong. They are resolved to save the precious period, pitifully short, from being wasted entirely by youthful vitality. The fact that they admit they must "interest" their pupils shows that they have, instinctively, the rudiments of good teaching approach. If the lesson does not hold the attention, then something is wrong. So these teachers use the only way they know—anything to keep them quiet.

Interest is an elusive thing. All persons are interested largely in that with which they have become familiar, by repeated contacts. But catching and holding the *attention* of anyone is a special art, often learned only the hard way. Interest is deep and belongs to the depths of character and the long years of cumulative experience. But attention is of the moment, yet calculated to touch the permanent interests, divert them to new channels. Thus, many a teacher may be able to command the attention of his class, but only repeated comradeship, and the long months of fellow-studying produce a deep interest.

Catching the attention usually calls for the use of the striking and the novel, since it must cut across the channels of established interests. Here are some of the devices for winning attention:

Dramatize yourself—tell personal experiences; adopt different roles, (impressive, vivacious, serious, sorry, etc.); use gestures, poses. These may be overdone, but there is not much danger, because we are usually far too restrained and speak and move in the same unchanging manner.

Use some striking *new touch*—change of voice, pace, silence; introduce a new object (book, article, cartoon); have pupils stand to recite. *Direct their gaze* to different things—the blackboard, open book, study passages, your gestures, finger-drills, etc. Let them talk about their experiences. This does not mean allowing them, or any one child, to dominate the period, but to bring some of their outside affairs into the class talk.

Study their reactions to your teaching. If they keep coming back for more, if they discuss the things you wish, accomplish the tasks you propose, then you have not only caught, in the hard-fought moments of teaching, their week-by-week attention, but you have won through to their interest. You will receive your reward when some day you hear a parent say, "John just can't miss your class. He says you are so interesting."

How to capture the continuing interest of boys is fundamentally not a bit different from how to interest girls. They are simply people, whose interests lie in the full tide of their daily lives, with which the good teacher is familiar and in sympathy. The same age-groups have about the same reactions in all parts of the world. Their attention is caught—or better, won, employed, *directed*—by the teacher who has learned how to stage-manage the class period. Such teachers come to realize that each session is a calculated dramatic performance which cannot depend solely on the inspiration of the moment any more than can a play on the stage. Back of it is much patient rehearsal.

11. PROBLEM TEACHERS

A pupil gets to be known as a "problem child" when he does not respond to ordinary handling. Under average conditions, most children do about what is expected of them, and, with variations, literally "do their duty in that state of life unto which it has pleased God to call them." They grow and flourish under conditions often not ideal and come through their schooling with credit to themselves.

Yet we all remember certain few children who, at some stage, stood out from the crowd and were a special problem—not bad enough to be dismissed, but erratic enough to give their superiors anxiety. They are the ones who spoil the fun of teaching, give teachers their moods of despair, annoyance, and exasperation. Such children have driven teachers to desperation, even to the thought of resigning. Sometimes they have required such a vast amount of time, patience, and special attention that the teacher has been tempted to declare, "It isn't fair—to me or to the class!" or even "I'm through."

But . . . in a flash of imagination, place yourself in the shoes of the rector or the superintendent of your school. (This is known as applying the Golden Rule.) Now look over the list of teachers in your parish school. Most of them are reliable, faithful, and successful—in a word, normal. Some few even are super-normal, the truly wonderful teachers, whom to know is to have a special door into the Christian religion. There remain the few who, by their irregular performance, must be classed as problem teachers—not bad enough to be dismissed, but erratic enough to give their superiors anxiety.

In short, there are always some teachers who are a problem to the parish authorities. They fall into a few types, very similar to the types of problem children:

(1) *The spoiled teacher*—He has had everything done for him, resents the slightest inconvenience, finds it difficult to teach unless every condition is exactly right. He blows up if the class next to his is noisy, if his material is not ready, if pupils get out of hand.

(2) *The lazy teacher*—He considers teaching easy, so never gets up his lesson. He reads from the book in class, never accomplishes the memory work, never asks for outside work. His box is never tidy, his table left in confusion at the close of the class.

(3) *The sensitive teacher*—He resents the slightest criticism, even when well merited, and wants praise for his most ordinary efforts; wants to be appreciated, he often hints broadly, for his sacrifices.

(4) *The old-fashioned teacher*—This one is still trying to employ the methods he recalls from his childhood parish. He may do one or two things well, but his mind is set against the modern ways of projects, discussions, self-expression, and pupil activity. He refuses to try out new materials.

(5) *The discouraged teacher*—He believes it can't be done: the children just don't respond. Parents don't care, he says, and the times are all against us. He has ceased to try very hard any more. Often absent or tardy.

(6) *The talkative teacher*—At first you like his glib enthusiasm, but soon notice that the children are getting restless and bored. The notebooks are found to have the same wording, because the sentences have been dictated. A written test reveals that the pupils have absorbed little.

(7) *The Low Church (or High) teacher*—He is bent on putting over his predilections in opposition to the established norm of the parish. Perhaps a splendid teacher, otherwise, but you can never be sure when he may undermine the rector's teaching by a dogmatic assertion of his own.

As with problem children, something can always be done about each one. The head of the school (like the teacher of the class) must work out a solution for each case. People can change, although sometimes it seems as though we are not the ones to accomplish it, and life is too short. All the above problem teachers can be transformed by skilful attention. (Possibly the last case is most fraught with difficulty, because the whole subject is tinged with emotion, and the rector cannot himself act dispassionately and objectively. If incurable, the teacher may have to be removed before he abuses his position of authority as a teacher.)

How? Look back over the list: The *spoiled teacher* needs to be given responsibility, the deepening experience of sharing in the school's planning and problems. The *lazy teacher* can be tactfully guided to greater zeal, inspired to better motives, sterner efforts, helped to experience the joy of success. The *sensitive teacher* deserves more recognition and will thrive on it. All of them will respond to personal conferences each month, to regular interest in their work, to constructive criticism, instead of being left so completely alone. Everyone who has a preconceived notion about his work can be reached, and his methods modified by tactful approach, by being given the right books. They all need encouragement, better materials, wise guidance, prompt help when they are in a jam, and frequent contact with an experienced and enthusiastic parish leader.

Maybe *you* are a problem teacher, and have recognized yourself in this list. And if alert, you will know part of the solution.

VI. CERTAIN TEACHING SKILLS

1. THE ART OF QUESTIONING

When a teacher complains, "My pupils don't seem to be very responsive," it may well be a sign that he has never caught on to the use of provocative questioning. Such a teacher may have slipped into the habit of telling—that is, lecturing. It is a habit that may be overcome by deliberately trying to provoke some response, not only from the few bright ones, but from all.

The classic form is the rhetorical question used in all oratory or speech addressed to a group. "Do you wish to be slaves forever?" "I ask you, recall your own youth, and tell me, can you blame this boy?" "Are you willing to give less to your Church than you spend for cigarettes?" The answers to all of these are obvious. They are all calculated to stimulate some response, either by spoken words, or of an inward forming of the reply, "No!"

Teachers should practice the use of questions. One good way is to fix in your mind some stock forms for phrasing a question which may easily be used again and again. Here are a few to have up your sleeve:

"What was the name of the man ————?" (*Factual.*)

"If you were (Zachaeus) how would you have felt when Jesus spoke to you?" (*Imaginative interpretation.*)

"This next question is for Helen, but if she cannot answer it, I want hands." (*To draw out the shy, yet hold the attention of the group.*)

"Where could we find out. . . . ?" (*Research stimulated; resources from beyond the class.*)

Many lessons have set questions printed at the end. Some teachers think these are to be read aloud, and a complete and satisfactory answer found for each. They had better be considered merely as attempts of the editor to assist the teacher in covering the main points. But the teacher may better prepare her own questions in advance, in writing, to make the discussion move better. These will seldom be read out just as they were written, but will be modified as the talk takes shape.

A very important part of lesson preparation should be this thinking out of possible questions. While experienced teachers do this easily, and skill comes from experience, some people are so temperamentally alert to the responsiveness of others that their whole conversation bristles with questions, or provocative expressions. That is why some classes are always happily "talking back," while others seem chronically sluggish. It is in the subtle difference between sentences that are barbed, stimulating, and that get under the skin, and that flow of words which reaches the ears but never penetrates the mind.

Here are a few suggestions:

Raise a problem: "How would we build a house if we lived in the Holy Land?" Don't tell them. Let their suggestions arise. Don't be in a hurry; this takes some time.

Wait for an answer: Some teachers never even expect an answer, and so kill the good of their questioning. Pause after the question. If there is a long silence, you had better rephrase it, or pass to something else.

Meet their minds: The question must be within the knowledge of your children, and in their own vocabulary, and be within their kind of experience. "How many of you have ever seen a live donkey?"

Don't encourage guessing: The teacher who promptly supplies the correct answer, particularly in factual review, is really stifling the interest. But if you keep demanding an answer when obviously no one knows it, you only start them guessing, which wastes time.

Use the blackboard: Often a single question may be written before the class assembles. Thus: "When did the Apostles discover that our Lord was the Son of God?" Teacher calls attention to the question at the start of class, remarking, "We may be able to answer that when we have studied the lesson for today." (Peter's confession at Caesarea Philippi.) The words on the board look down on the class during the development of the story, and finally serve as the summary of the day's thought.

Ask for opinions: Questions may be worded to draw out personal reaction. This form may often be requested in writing, and the various compositions of the class read for discussion.

Let the teacher who senses a lack of response from his class try to prepare several carefully worded questions to fit his next week's lesson. Plan to use them through the lesson, not just at the end. It may change one's whole method and success in teaching.

2. THE ART OF DRILL

To drill means to do something over and over until it is known perfectly, and can be done again, when called for. For certain permanent knowledge there is no substitute for drill. We must train our children in certain fundamental skills, movements, attitudes, responses, and definitions if they are to be effective Churchmen, useful soldiers of Christ, when the need comes. The great difficulty in most Church Schools is that there is so little time, with the result that there is a new lesson each week, which is seldom referred to again. Things come to the front of the child's consciousness for a day, are not recalled or used, and so are completely forgotten.

There is an immediate advantage in drill in teaching obedience, attention, and specific information. But we must also keep in our minds that the things we teach our children now are their spiritual equipment for life. If they don't learn certain things, now, so thoroughly that those things are a part of them, it is very likely they never will. There is altogether too much vague, inaccurate, and half-remembered knowledge among adults.

Methods of drill in the classroom differ, but they all work to the one end: that every pupil shall know, for life-long use, the essentials of the material being studied. He must be able to *give it back,* in class, and many years later. In spite of discoveries that we can memorize late in life, the truth remains that we seldom do.

"I am grateful to my old teacher," remarked a woman, "that she made me learn the 23rd Psalm and the 91st. They have been reservoirs of strength when I needed something definite to say in my devotions."

It is possible to make the repetition of drill a pleasure by ingenious games. This is easier to do than you would suppose, but it does take some advance thought and preparation. The main principle is to use the group for some form of mild competition. Although learning is always a personal matter, yet in class it is done in companionship with others and with the stimulus of display and approval by your group. The familiar Step Catechism, by which a page at a time is learned and signed by the leader, is of this type. The following are some kinds and methods of drill that have proved effective. For memorizing long sections, a variety of these methods will make the drill more pleasant:

(1) *Silent study*—having found the item in the book, the class memorizes it until the teacher calls them to attention again, asking individuals to recite. In Church School, with our

precious forty minutes or less, this may be from five to eight minutes.

(2) *Class recites in concert*—This was the general method in all ancient schools, and still has much value. It is the way most Churchmen, over the years, learn hymns, psalms, and the words of the Prayer Book.

(3) *Blackboard*—Use a blackboard or memory chart for all to read, either silently or in concert. (A set of such cards, to hang on the wall, containing the prescribed memory work for a given course, may be the next adjunct for an alert publisher to produce.)

(4) *Home study*—The passage is given out to be *learned at home*. This saves much class time, and has the advantage of requiring the parents to be a party with the school. After home study, however, it is requisite that time for recitation be given and every individual checked up. Otherwise such home assignments soon fall off, since there is no recognition after the work has been done. It means that the teacher will have to be at church some time before the opening, to hear individual reports and recitation, and often linger after for the same purpose.

It is the responsibility of every teacher to keep a record of the exact learning achievements of each pupil, or results will diminish. Without such a checkup, the marks or rewards that go with it will have small effect. For example, every Scoutmaster has his little book in which he checks the progress of every boy: pledge, scout law, flag, etc. No Scout passes to the next step until he has done completely each requirement.

Some Useful Drills

On finding places in the Bible (about fourth grade and after). Make it a contest, boys *vs.* girls. Or put the list on the board, requiring each child to find the verse in his Bible, writing down the first two words of the text to prove he was correct.

On the use of a concordance. For this, Bibles with concordance or topical index must be used, or enough separate concordances supplied for the whole class. Problems are given, and the book, chapter, and verse are to be located. Thus: Find the verse about the burning bush; the story about Jairus' daughter; "my grace is sufficient"; St. Paul's address on Mar's Hill; the raising of Lazarus, etc.

On finding "propers" (Collect, Epistle, and Gospel) for the day, in Prayer Book. Should be done frequently, without any help, and with perfect accuracy.

On the use of tables in front of Prayer Book: The date of Easter for any given year, and the major feasts for any year. How to use the monthly calendars as perpetual calendars, locating the Sunday letter for any given year. This is loads of fun, once the teacher has learned how himself. For instance, by this you can find out the day of the week on which you were born.

On finding the special psalms for a Sunday, or a special day.

On finding the Bible lessons for any day, morning or evening. Thus, write on board, "Find 2nd lesson in Morning Prayer for the Tuesday after the Fifteenth Sunday after Trinity."

On the order of events or topics in various categories. For this sets of cards or slips are made, to be shuffled and then arranged in the correct sequence. This applies to such as the following:

The order of places in the Prayer Book. Set of cards with titles of the different sections—Calendar, Morning Prayer, etc.

The order of the clauses in the creed.

The order of the events in the Life of Christ.

The order of principal events in Church history.

The advantage of all the above is not only in the learning which is accomplished by repetition under pleasant motivation, but in the ease with which such drills can be introduced into the lesson period. Whenever things seem to be going badly, or the material has played out too soon, the teacher who has some of these drills prepared can always turn to them in an instant and save the session.

There are a number of useful card games to be had from publishers, but they are of unequal value. It is far better to make your own card games. For example, you decide to make a drill set on symbolism. You secure about twenty 4″ x 6″ cards, plain white. Some catalogs of Church furnishings houses are brought to class, and pictures of a stole, chalice, lectern, etc., cut out and pasted on one side of each card. On the back is printed by hand the name and use of the article. In use, one pupil holds the card toward another, showing the picture. "What is this?" he asks, and the other must reply with the name and its use. Similar sets can be readily made for living missionary bishops, for sets of pictures on the Life of Christ, or for key dates in Church history. Another way to use these is to have the cards bear a number, tack them around the room, and have class go about, identifying each on tally sheet. This is always a pleasant change. Such sets can be loaned to other classes, may be used over and over.

In all drill, the teacher is the real problem. Teachers who are patient and thorough, and who appreciate the great importance of drill, will plan and put some of it into every lesson. Those who are casual, who have no long plan or hopes for their pupils, will probably go on talk-talking to restive pupils, who will have little to show in after life for their year spent in that class.

3. HOW TO LEAD A DISCUSSION PERIOD

When several people talk together for awhile, something happens. Not only does each person express himself (which gives him a certain pleasure and satisfaction), but he contributes something of value—his opinion, and possibly some information. When all have spoken, there comes a stage of assimilation. Everyone gets something from the contributions of the others, either to modify or strengthen his own position. Even the most opinionated is swayed, a little. The shy one finds his theory, his scrap of information, an acceptable contribution to the meeting.

But that is not all. Something new is created in a discussion time, even when not planned or anticipated, which could never otherwise have come into being. The result is not simply the total of all information and ideas; it is a new thing, the developing, common mind of a group of persons acting upon each other. This is the great value of discussion, whether in classes, or committees, or congresses. It creates something. It really accomplishes something, and often starts plans and developments not expected.

There are dangers. A discussion, even though you "stick to your subject," may degenerate into a mere expression of prejudices, or a mouthing of the current shallow "public opinion." To go around the circle asking, "And what do *you* think about this?" may prove to be only the pumping of many empty wells. Very much depends on the skill and preparation and purpose of the leader.

To watch a skilled discussion leader drawing out everyone, developing a theme, injecting new material, then leading the talk into a profitable conclusion, may look very simple. But be not misled. This is one of the highest of the arts of teaching, and, along with story-telling and drill, an essential skill for teachers of any age pupils. You can (and should) employ it from the kindergarten circle through the graduate seminar. Digest these rules and techniques, practice them for a while, and you will begin to enjoy exhilarating results.

(1) Establish personal contact quickly. Put your class or group at ease. This applies especially to older groups, when the leader may be slightly self-conscious. Never speak about yourself, and never apologize for having accepted the place as leader; dive right in and *be* the leader. Make your first words attractive, vivacious, confident. Plan your opening well. The more selfless you are, the quicker will the meeting develop a self of its own.

The poor leader does it this way: "Now, I hope you'll all feel free to ask questions. . . . I'm new at this, you know . . . I'm just the leader. I hope you'll all talk right up. . . ." Then he talks vaguely for another ten minutes, and still no one says a word. He is getting rattled. It's terrible. What shall he do?

(2) It is best here to state the main topic of the meeting or class-period briefly. "Today we are going to talk about family budgeting. You will all have something to contribute, I'm sure. And we have an expert present who can give us some information about trends in prices. At the end of the discussion, perhaps we may reach some interesting conclusions." That's about enough. Perhaps a few more sentences, just to make sure the stage is set and there is no misunderstanding. But by all means avoid a long preliminary statement.

(3) Now, to start talk from the floor, pose a simple question, and ask for a solution or opinion. This has to be very carefully thought out. It should not call for a mere yes-or-no answer. State the question clearly, and then *pause*. In the pause, let your eye run along the faces in the front rows. (If you keep on talking, you only kill the chance for a response.) If no one

speaks up voluntarily, which is most likely, point suddenly to some likely looking person in front and say, "You." The person is bound to give some reply, and your discussion is under way. This first question should not be the main theme, just a subsidiary one, probably very obvious. Don't linger long over it. It is intended only to point their minds, and get started.

A variation of this is to walk at once to the blackboard and write something provocative, such as, "Qualities Required in a Successful Missionary." Turn, face group, chalk poised. Look in every eye—pause. Call on an individual, or give chalk to some one. Don't prolong this, but use as a starter for response.

(4) Work to get several more individuals talking, as soon as possible. One over-talkative person may have to be put down politely, to get the more timid ones into it. Keep asking leading questions, or changing the wording. Even some disagreement at this stage is a lucky break, because it develops the topic.

(5) You must now get beyond mere opinions and introduce some concrete information, some facts to chew on. Therefore, read a short statement, or call for a few pre-arranged reports. "I have asked Lucia to summarize a clipping on the work of Quakers during the war." Or, "Harry is going to tell us how many churches and communicants we have in Puerto Rico."

(6) Have an agenda, memorized or on a card. But don't reveal it too rapidly. You might have a rough timing noted, to guide you. The meeting must *seem* to take its own lead, to be spontaneous and original.

(7) Let the meeting pursue any side issues that arise, but, as the leader, keep calling them back to your main objective.

(8) Have plenty of reserve ammunition—stories, anecdotes, cases, quotations, statistics. Don't use these unless necessary. Matter contributed from the group is often much more vital.

(9) At an early stage, appoint a secretary to note down any point you wish to call up later. This is often better than the

blackboard. Note any outcomes that begin to arise, referring them to the secretary as "things we might decide to do about this." This is the "project" method. The secretary's notes are reviewed near the end, and if one or two plans are approved, a person or committee may be asked to carry them further.

(10) All through the discussion, you must never antagonize, never argue. You must be an impartial leader, not a private individual putting over your own notions. Your sole purpose is to lead persons to vibrate to a theme. Sometimes the violent disagreement of one person will clinch most effectively the right view of all the rest. You may win your one maverick later, or in private. After all, truth is not a voting matter, but one of discovery, realization, and assimilation.

(11) As you see that your time is running out, summarize briefly, and try to get something started, some individuals to promise to do something before next time.

(12) Stop the meeting while it is still interesting. A few may remain to talk further, but the formal meeting should be dismissed. You want the group to have a pleasant impression, and to come back for more, don't you?

Make these twelve rules your own. Practice them intelligently and often, and you will find that your classes and meetings always are vital. You may become known as the great leader.

4. GAMES IN CLASS

Decent novelty will save any class from settling down into a boresome monotony. If you will always remember the point of view of the children, you will frequently plan for differing kinds of activity in class. Some teachers temperamentally are ingenious, sense the dramatic, and know when to switch to something that is more fun.

Here are five games and drills which may be used in class at almost any time, provided they are well thought-out, launched with the right preliminaries.

(1) *Places in Prayer Book*—The class or department is lined up as in the old-fashioned spell-down. Pupils who miss go to the bottom. In the closing round those who miss drop out, and the survivor is the winner. Leader has prepared a long list of questions such as: How many lessons in Morning Prayer? From what part of the Bible is the First Lesson taken? In what service do we hear the Comfortable Words? What comes after Baptism?—after Evening Prayer?—after the Creed in Holy Communion? Where do you find Family Prayer?

Variation: With Prayer Books in hand, allowing 20 seconds to find the answer: What is the Epistle for Septuagesima? On what page is the table for Easter? etc.

(2) *To Stimulate Original Expression*—A teacher of young people found this worked well: First, slips were given out on which were typed significant statements of Jesus' teachings. These were numbered, and, after some opening remarks by the leader, each was called upon to comment on his slip. Would it work today? Do many people really believe this?

Then a second set of slips was given out, arranged as follows: The leader held complete set of questions. Two duplicate sheets had been cut up and handed among the class, one of each marked with a red circle, the other with a blue. Leader calls on "Red" to give his opinion, then asks "Blue" if he agrees, or not. Success of this method depends a great deal on the selection and careful wording of the questions.

(3) *Church Vocabulary*—This device lasts all year. A large scrap-book or manila sketch-book with spiral binding. Teacher opens the book, has crayon in hand, writes "A" at top, draws line down middle of page—boys' words to be written on one side, girls' on the other. Two sides call out words alternately,

thus: Advent, altar, amice, aisle, angel. If the meaning of the word can't also be explained, it doesn't count.

Next week, after showing the former page for quick review, "B" is written, and names starting with that letter suggested. The game lasts all year as the alphabet is covered. It arouses great interest, and may be used as the basis for a written review. For this review a list of words used in the game is typed, and pupils are asked to write a short definition or identify each by some phrase.

(4) *Make Your Own Card Games*—We are familiar with the card games sold by Church publishers. The best type have a picture or graph on one side, question and answer on the other.*

(5) *Parts of The Prayer Book*—The Prayer Book (like the Bible) is really a number of books bound together. To make this clear, teacher comes prepared with nine slips or cards, on the end of each of which is written the name of one part of the Prayer Book: Calendars, Morning Prayer, Evening Prayer, Prayers and Thanksgivings, Litany, Holy Communion, Occasional Offices, Psalter, Ordinal (plus Family Prayer, Articles?). In use, a pupil is given a Prayer Book, asked to insert each slip in proper place—sticking out—at the start of each section. Or, the slips may simply be shuffled, and the requirement is to arrange in the correct order. A similar set of slips may be made for the parts of a single service. For drill on learning books of the Bible, type names on sheet, cut up, and ask to have pieces arranged in correct order.

In all use of such games, the teacher should be sure to repeat the drills to impress the facts covered. The element of competition arouses keen interest. Caution: use these for the end of the period, never at the start, as they are great time users, and often only the bell can stop them.

* See description of method of making these in Chapter 2, "The Art of Drill," page 165.

5. STORY-TELLING TECHNIQUES

The telling of stories ranks among the foremost skills of teaching. Moreover, to be able to tell stories effectively, in any social group, gives one a pleasure and a position that is unique. The story-teller has a place and a power; this has been true from the dawn of history. No one is too old to be interested by a story. The following are some methods which have been helpful to others.

(1) Before you begin to prepare, *set the stage* in your mind. Visualize vividly the scene and setting in which you are to tell this story. Picture your class in its circle, yourself facing them. Every eye is upon you. (Resolve not to let any slight embarrassment, or the use of notes, cause you to lose contact with one of those eyes.) Now, don't let the thought get you in a panic of your old shyness. You are going out on a stage, but before an audience that is friendly and appreciative, not critical. It is going to be your big moment. And it is going to be fun! Finally, review in a flash—for the hundredth time—the special age, needs, responses, of your particular pupils. They are your public, your only audience. For them alone you prepare.

(2) To tell a story, you must know the story well. That's fundamental. This does not mean to memorize it, but know it. The safest and simplest way is to read it through three times. Never trust your quick mind and memory with a "once over." Never be overconfident. So, read the story through twice at the first attack. Then, after a little while—perhaps after some hours of other study or activity, or if possible a day or more later—read it through again.

(3) Then *set up* the story in your own mind. What comes first, what next, what then? What are the high spots, what the ending? Some teachers do this in a systematic way with a writ-

ten outline. More just straighten the material out in their mind, run over it a few times to make sure they have it all.

(4) Here, you might *improve* on the story. It comes to you in the printed form—in textbook or Bible—which you have just read over. But the writer might not have done justice to the underlying story. There are two ways you can always polish a story:

First, point up the *characterization*. Think of every person who appears in the story, one by one. Decide on some details of appearance and personality for each. Thus: "The farmer met Emily. . . ." (original story.) Your improvement on this: "Down the road came the tall farmer in patched blue overalls. As he stopped in front of Emily she saw there was a merry twinkle in his eye." If you *see* these details, you will readily get them into your story, when you finally tell it; you need not decide on the exact wording.

Give every character a name or descriptive title or adjective, and call him by this name or title every time he appears. This will not sound monotonous, and aids in keeping the story clear in the minds of the listeners.

Second, put in a lot of conversation and *direct quotations*. Thus: (weak) "one of the disciples told Jesus there was a boy. . . ." How much better the Bible does it: "Andrew (Simon Peter's brother) said to Jesus, 'There is a lad here who has five . . .'"

Try this method with any story. Without writing anything down (for that might make the effect stiff, and the whole process a burden) *make up* complete conversations, with direct words in the mouths of all your characters. Never mind if they are not in very fine wording. They will be alive, and the imaginations of your young listeners will make up for any lack of literary polish.

Just to fix this last elementary principle in your mind, it is usually expressed: *avoid indirect discourse.* Place all possible words in the mouths of persons in the story. As one old teacher expressed it, "Use more quotes." For example: "Jesus . . . asked him what he wanted." (This is indirect discourse.) St. Luke was a better story-teller, for he wrote it, "Jesus asked, 'What wilt thou that I should do unto thee?' "

You may, indeed, have to apply this principle to amplifying the Bible text. Remember, the Gospels are clipped, often far too brief, and we have a right to expand them if we do not change their real meaning. For example, "They rebuked the blind man that he should hold his peace" (St. Luke 18:39). You may decide to tell this: "The people around said to him, 'Be quiet! You're making too much noise!' "

Then, too, you may wish to invent more conversation to sustain the dramatic action. For example, one teacher expanded the story about like this:

"The blind man asked, 'What is all that noise?'

"His friends said, 'It is a great crowd coming along the road.'

"The blind man asked, 'Why is there such a crowd?'

"They answered, 'Jesus of Nazareth is passing by.'

"Then the blind man began to shout, 'Jesus, Jesus,' etc."

(5) Your *bodily actions* are important. You may shrink from the thought of making gestures, yet anyone, no matter how awkward or shy, can add to a story by some simple motions. If you are one who feels a little self-conscious about this, the following is suggested: Run over the story mentally to see if you can imitate a few of the obvious movements of the characters. Of course you may have to tell the story while seated, but you can do a lot with your head and hands. Thus: "He held out his hands. He looked up to heaven. He saw him in the tree. He shivered in the cold." Surely you can do the action suggested by each of these.

But *think out* the gesture, and even practice it, as part of your preparation. You can readily draw pictures by gestures. Thus: "He came toward them down the winding road" (point, movement of wrist). "The city had walls with square towers" (sketch the sky-line of city with hand in air). "The arrow shot out and fell" (curving motion). Try it. It's easier than you think.

There's more to story-telling than all this. But you can work at it and get better rapidly, if you will. Of course, you are not going to tell stories all the time, or you wouldn't be doing any teaching. Nor are you likely (if you are a skillful teacher) to tell a different story every single Sunday. That would be falling into one of the many fixed patterns which so often make teaching monotonous. But you will be telling and re-telling stories, to one group or another, all your life, and you owe it to yourself and your work to become expert in it.

6. HOW TO MEMORIZE

We have all noticed that some children can memorize things easier and quicker than others. There are various opinions and theories why this is so. Some people can go over a passage to be learned with such intensity of attention that the words seem to etch themselves upon their minds with a few efforts.

With others we notice their attack. They *go at* a learning assignment in a moment, without any hesitation or "stalling around." They have truly well disciplined minds, willing quickly to do something, and being on the job the next instant.

Again, it is partly a matter of confidence. Those who have learned hard bits in the past know that they can do it, and so approach new assignments with a feeling that it's easy.

One such student comes to my mind. He was given a part in a pageant in an emergency, and was handed his script even as the first act was starting. While the costume was being fitted on him, he worked at his lines, asking only, "Don't talk to me, I'm memorizing." When he came on, not 20 minutes later, he knew every line of a rather long scene, and even prompted another actor. This boy had a ready mind, but he had done such feats before, and knew that he could do it, easily.

Now, as it concerns us as teachers, there are two main parts to memorization—motive and method.

"I could do it if I wanted," is the explanation of many a child when twitted that he can't throw, or jump, or sing, or do one of the many activities of the school. That is the secret spring of every life, were the truth known—if I wanted to! How to make the child want is the leader's real problem.

Memorizing set words is a natural activity, in which every living person, including the lowest forms of mentality, may compete. Anyone can memorize. Tests prove that, literally, we are never too old to learn.

Growing children, using their minds, like their bodies, experimentally, are delighted to discover that they can memorize. It gives them pleasure for several reasons. One is the sheer joy of achievement. This is one of life's deepest joys.

A girl of fourteen was found to be learning the Nicene Creed. She was asked, "Did your teacher assign that?", and replied, "Oh, no, it was the Apostles' Creed, but I knew that already, and just learned the Nicene for fun." We teachers should never forget that it is fun to learn, once started, and we deprive our pupils of a great experience if we do not help them in it.

Besides the joy of doing it, there is more commonly the motive of pride and exhibition. We recite our piece to be heard by the class or audience. We do it, mildly, to show off. But we do it, and thereby the material is in our minds, ready for later use. Let it be said here, teachers who personally find memorizing distasteful will not get good results from their class. Such teachers will not be as apt to start their pupils on a new assignment with enthusiasm.

Doubtless the best urge to learn is for immediate use. This applies naturally to lines in a play, to prayers to be said in real devotions. Another consideration is the kind of material. Some will find verse easiest, while others can master prose more readily. Unfamiliar and meaningless matter is always learned more slowly. But always, the teacher must keep the class at their work, and each accomplishes the assignment by contagious leadership.

Memorizing is accomplished either in class or at home. Many teachers who labor faithfully to make the memory period of the class fruitful fail to make any assignments for home work. Indeed, here is where we all miss an ever present opportunity. Parents and children respect the teacher who sends home a typed slip "To be memorized before next Sunday." Expect results and you will get them.

Class methods of drill are various, and the ingenious teacher makes up her own. There are the visual, using the book, blackboard or flash cards;* the choral, reciting in concert; and the

---

* Flash cards are readily made by hand, and speed memory work a great deal. Get several pieces of white cardboard about 10 x 12 inches, or whatever size fits the class and item to be learned. On this, copy the passage on one side with crayon or black ink. (A different assignment may be on each side, requiring fewer cards.) Punch hole at center of top, and fasten loop of string. A class of four or five can sit closely together so that they can use smaller cards, with lettering not over half inch high. For larger class, make chart of a size to be read across the room, with letters about three-fourths of an inch high. Two uses:

(1) *For the whole class:* Hang card on wall. Class recites in concert. Then individuals try. The child reciting faces the class, his back to the card, while the others watch to detect mistakes. When any one has recited it perfectly, he is permitted to write his name on the margin. The cards are kept hanging on the wall, and are always available for quick drill.

(2) *For personal drill:* There are several cards, made smaller. Two children work on one card. One holds it up, lettering towards partner, who reads it aloud. Holder then turns the blank side, keeping his own eye on the script while partner recites. Thus slight errors are caught at once, and the correct way established.

pupil-leader, where the child who has already learned the section takes charge and calls for others to recite.

One proven psychological principle may be taught older children, asked to learn long passages. The rule is: Don't learn one line or verse at a time. Instead, read over the entire passage, again and again. Oddly enough, progress will seem to be slower by the latter method. But if you will stick to it, you can actually master the whole section with less repetition, in shorter time. And it will stay in your mind more permanently.

Teachers, a personal tip: Take up memorizing as a pastime, for your own pleasure. It will give you a sense of mental power you have not realized for years, and (if you memorize the right things) it will enable you to give great pleasure to others, at unexpected moments.

7. THE VALUE OF MEMORIZING

I am eternally grateful to the Chicago public school system for inspiring me (or compelling me, I suspect) to memorize, "The quality of mercy is not strained," "What is so rare as a day in June?" and other gems of my literary inheritance. They come in mighty handy at times.

I am also grateful to my boyhood parish for seeing that I learned, about the same time, "Come, Holy Ghost, our souls inspire," besides "And now our Eucharist is o'er, Yet for one blessing still we plead. . . ." These treasures I have recalled literally thousands of times. They are part of me, and they have helped me grow in the Faith. With such things ready in my mind, I have been able to teach others. Without them, I would be a poor and ill-equipped Christian.

The value of exact and beautiful passages held in the mind, and used at will, is readily recognized. Facts, lists, details of

stories, names, dates, definitions, and the like are the common
grist of school learning. These have their place, it is true, in the
total volume of human knowledge. But the *use* of such matter
(except in the long chance of your being called up at a radio
quiz program) in adult life is very slight. The things to memorize which will be of use all through life are the devotional
and spiritual passages through which we may express ourselves
and refresh our souls. You either have a store of these in your
mind, from childhood days, or you don't. Few people, unless
especially inclined, will be apt to memorize late in life.

It is therefore our special responsibility to see that our boys
and girls actually learn certain choice and tested selections from
our Christian literary resources. Some of these, it is true, will
be accomplished without special effort, by natural repetition
in use at our services. These things include the creeds, the
Lord's Prayer, and many frequently sung hymns. There is a
further list of memory gems which should be the common
property of all Christians, but which no one is apt to have
learned unless directed and held to the task by a teacher. Here
is the special field of the Church School and class.

There are two theories, it should be noted, as to the use of
verbal memorizing in Christian education. The one extreme is
the ancient method which looked upon all knowledge as a
transmission of the ancient words, to be learned exactly, with
little stress upon the understanding. Picture an ancient class of
oriental boys (girls didn't have any such advantages) sitting on
the floor, droning aloud the endless scripture they were memorizing. From them it is a long jump to the other extreme of a
modern Sunday School where a little class is seated around a
table in the parish house, cheerfully emoting and evolving some
project in self-expression. The boys of old could and did recite
their lines all their lives. In contrast, the modern children frequently "have nothing to show for their time," (as Grandfather

grumps) except a few bits of novel handwork and some pleasant impressions.

In between these two extremes of all-memorizing and no-memorizing—entire verbalization and complete self-expression—lies the whole field of varied and effective teaching. On this middle ground, indeed, may yet be fought to its inconclusive finish the war between the Authoritarians ("Christianity is revealed, transmitted Truth: know it") and the Vitalitarians ("Religion is Life: live it"). There seems to be no discharge in that war, once you have taken sides, unless, at long last, we may discover that objective and subjective are only head and tail of the same precious coin of life.

The reader may feel that the foregoing is largely theory, but it comes home to him, if a teacher, in the decision to make much or little of memorization, and what things are to be memorized. Granted that you hope to give your pupils something permanently useful, for all of life, what shall these things be? One method, which held the field for several generations, and may still be seen in some old-fashioned courses, is the "golden text" which was memorized, one for each Sunday. Thus, a year's achievement was to know all fifty-two of the texts letter-perfect. Since the same texts were often used again, year after year, the memory equipment of such children was often just this list of selected single verses from the Bible. These often were rich in evangelical meaning, but also were often key texts calling for a large theological knowledge for their complete understanding. Many oldsters can thus recall or recognize many texts which for them are old friends, but which as often have little real meaning.

Another system, of about the same period, was also based on the Sunday-by-Sunday method, and attempted the learning of the collect for the day. This may still be found the practice in certain English and Canadian parishes, and in our country

where there is a great emphasis on the Prayer Book. The knowledge of the collects is certainly of more value than separate
texts. But it is difficult to learn a new collect each Sunday, and
younger children are not ready for them. Moreover, such a rigid
scheme leaves out many other kinds of memory items.

Let us approach this question of what to memorize in the
Church School by seeing what we desire at the end of our
system. Here is a young adult, who has been through our parish
course and is now twenty to thirty years old. Just what things
can he recite from memory because we have taught him?

In the first place, for what occasions in life have we prepared
him? He surely should have ready some appropriate words for
such times as these: His daily night and morning prayers, with
enough variations to fit all kinds of personal problems; some
prayers at noon; some ejaculatory prayers to say while busy;
a grace at meals; prayers for and with a sick person; a prayer
for opening any meeting; beautiful passages for comfort or
inspiration, to be said for personal uplift, or to help others.
Some of these latter will include choice psalms, hymns, and
Bible passages.

The selection of the items to be taught to meet this intended
use is one of the foremost problems of the Church's curriculum
planning. There should be a memory schedule, with electives
and variations, which should be set up and followed year after
year. Certain minimum and some extra things should be listed.
Up to the present, no such complete list has been set forth. Each
teacher, at the start of the year's work, will have to make up
her own scheme, and try to accomplish it, through the year.
It's too bad, but at present the teacher, possibly with the help
of the priest, must do this alone. Since both have their hobbies
and limitations, it is a frail foundation.

Happy will be the Church which, from a competent head-
quarters, and after years of experiment, holds up an official list

of things which must be memorized. The second strand of the old Christian Nurture Series, "Memory Work," was a thoughtful effort to carry through this year-long planning.

Considering again our end-result, in the graduate of our school, we can list the main requirements of such a list, which may some day be promulgated by authority. This list would include:

The creeds, the Lord's Prayer, and the Ten Commandments, surely, before we branch out on the many other things which a Christian ought to know and believe to his soul's health.

A few devotional hymns—mostly objective (to and about God), but some subjective, though not sentimental. Certain others poems (for older students) from our English classics, having devotional value. These last are often learned in literature classes at school or college, but seldom at church.

Certain carefully selected collects and other prayers to fit definite occasions, as given above.

Some devotions to use at the Eucharist.

Two or three psalms.

A few other golden passages, not too short, from the Bible.

A few definitions from the Catechism.

Once such a list is made, the teacher will have a special duty to see that her pupils know the items assigned for that year and to drill on those learned in the preceding year.

After the teacher has adopted or been given such a list of objectives, there remains the problem of inducing the children to learn them. We all memorize only when we are motivated. Thus, the pupil may learn in order to get the signature on the page of his step-catechism (achievement); or to get his name on the honor roll (recognition, competition); or to be in a play or pageant (display); or just because his teacher's desire and enthusiasm are catching (contagious leadership).

Leave a place in each lesson-plan for memory drill. If you

don't, you may go weeks without accomplishing anything. Some teachers neglect it almost completely, and as a result their pupils are cheated of this part of their training.

Keep the class memorizing *together* as far as possible, but encourage the child with a flair for memorizing to master as much as he will in addition.

Learn the class's assignments yourself, letter-perfect. You simply cannot teach memorizing from a book or chart. This inspires confidence, makes it possible to drill at any moment, without looking up materials.

Above all, stick to it, for a part of each lesson; don't leave a lot of loose items only half memorized.

8. TEACHING WITH A FILMSTRIP*

Every teacher ought to know how to use the new miniature projectors by which small photographs, on single slides or strips of film, are thrown on a screen. The method is old (remember the old magic lantern?) but recent improvements and increasing use in education have given it a new prominence. There is a danger that churches buy the equipment without knowing how to fit it into the teaching program. Be it known that at present there is no such thing as a "program of visual education" in any sense that you can buy sets of pictures to illustrate every lesson of a course. The pictorial elements in the Bible have been studied by producers, and pictures made of nearly every scene in the life of Christ, and many in the Old Testament. But pictures alone do not convey religion, and their proper use by the teacher calls for careful study and preparation.

The simplest and most convenient form of transparency is

* The use of motion pictures is too large a subject for this book. The use of one type of picture projection is here described as a help to teachers, and to stress the *teaching* activity.

the filmstrip, which is recommended as a good way to start any church in the use of projected pictures. This is a piece of standard film about four feet long and with thirty or more single pictures which are shown one at a time. When you are through discussing a picture, you simply turn the knob of the projector to the next. When through, the little filmstrip is put back in its tiny box, ready for use by another class, or in other years. The cost is low, and a school gradually builds its library of strips. The filmstrips are increasingly being produced by both commercial and Church bodies, and may even be made by home talent.

After your school has bought the projector and some film strips or slides, teachers must know how to use them. It is easy to run the pictures through the machine, but to make of them a constructive educational experience is the problem. First, you must become acquainted with the strip or group of pictures you are to show. Don't be too sure you remember the story. You must know well every picture you are to show. This requires that you will have set up the projector the day before and run through the full sequence, jotting down notes as you go. You should at this time read the script usually provided by the makers with each strip, to be sure you get the full intent of the editors. But you must go beyond these notes, know as much as possible about the theme. And, if it is a filmstrip on a Biblical subject, be sure you re-read the Bible passage carefully.

The next step is to prepare the children. Before the pictures are shown, present the theme to the class or department which is later to see it, aiming to point their minds toward it, so that they will not be seeing entirely unfamiliar matter. Yet you should try to do this without "spoiling the surprise," or leaving nothing for the actual showing.

This preliminary talk by the leader takes place in the class the Sunday before the showing, either as a short statement, or in the form of a directed discussion, creating vital interest in the topic underlying the pictures. This may be part of the development of a class project. Thus, an older class is led into a discussion on "Dating," and you mention that you have some pictures entitled "Boy Meets Girl." Could we find time to examine them next Sunday?

Finally the filmstrip is shown, and the teacher has the problem of speaking while the pictures are thrown on the screen, in a nice balance between an informative lecture and planned questions aimed at student response. *This takes more careful preparation than ordinary teaching.*

Some teaching tips and cautions are given below. These will have much more meaning to you after you have used the projector a few times and realize some of the difficulties, as well as the great possibilities of the method:

(1) Your talk must fit the picture—don't merely give generalities recalled by it.

(2) Yet you must go beyond the picture with added information. On the other hand, brevity and movement are essential. Those who know *too* much are apt to tell it, and be boresome.

(3) Have your material organized, not just a lot of loose comment. Knowing the age pupils you will be addressing, you will have decided on their probable interests and will refer to some of their experiences as points of contact. Use simple but exact words.

(4) Avoid the obvious, merely identifying: "See the big camel."

(5) Work for student response and interpretation by carefully thought-out questions: Thus, "What is that in his hand?" "Billy, how do you think the shepherd felt?" "How many of these men are Pharisees, how many are disciples? Jane, go to the screen and point to them."

(6) Talk quietly and insist on perfect co-operation. Mischief

breaks out in the dark, and you must be ever-alert to control the tone and to maintain the pitch of interest. On the other hand, you will find that you gain in concentration of attention (if your talk is "clicking") because of the dark, with all eyes held by the screen, and the changing images.

(7) Show to small groups of nearly the same age, so your talk can fit their vocabulary and interests, and so you may have every one take part in the discussion.

(8) Have a separate projection space always set up, so as not to have to fuss with curtains, screen, and electric cords. This need be only a space large enough for about a dozen persons, where groups are taken in turn, by pre-arrangement.

(9) Have a separate operator, and if possible a special teacher who is prepared to present all the filmstrips in your library. Thus, the regular class teacher gives the pre-statement, by memorandum from the Projection Leader, then brings her class to the "Little Theater" at the time set. The Leader may soon be known as the "Story-Tell Lady."

(10) Keep your shows short, only a portion of the class period. Many filmstrips can be shown in twenty minutes. The class may then return to its own room or alcove to continue the lesson, or discuss the strip.

(11) Plan your showings, by a school schedule, weeks ahead, so that teachers may anticipate and fit them into their courses. This helps to keep them on their toes, and gives to the children a sense of something coming.

(12) Finally, let's keep this in perspective, as part of our normal teaching. What we want is activity, pupil response. The trouble with pictures is that on the whole they call for only passive attention. In spite of the ballyhoo, a picture is still only a picture, and our concern is primarily with *ideas* and their expression in lives. There are three stages or levels of teaching, from the lowest to the highest, in the following order:

First, *Words*—verbalizing of all sorts, listening, definitions, and catechisms.

Second, *Visual*—anything done or shown in the presence of the student which reaches him through his eyes. This includes gestures by teacher, blackboards, graphs, wall pictures, drawings, chromos, sketches, cartoons, illustrated leaflets, stereopticon slides, and now the 2 x 2 slides, filmstrips, movies, and sound-movies. The projection of pictures has swept the educational world, and reached the churches. One often suspects that the new interest is embraced in the hope of finding a short-cut to success, by some mechanized process, and perhaps as a substitute for reality—the subconscious which welcomes activity with *things* in the flight from the more difficult ultimate of dealing with *people*, that is, with our pupils. But visual aids are part of our program, and may be used if we know their relation to our real goals.

Third, *Activity*—This means any form of personal participation in a guided experience. Everything in our teaching should aim toward this. For example, the making of a poster involves *words, visual,* and *activity*; but the activity uses the first two and makes them live.

In your search for a personal hobby, this may be it! to make yourself the Visual Leader for your school, knowing all the equipment, training a staff, learning the techniques of presenting the pictures to each age-group, and perhaps being the official photographer who takes 35mm colored pictures of all classes, organizations and occasions, and shows them at appropriate times. Here is a real calling.

9. STUDENT NOTEBOOKS

Many teachers use student notebooks without knowing why. Few realize fully their possibilities and limitations. Writing is the simplest form of self-expression, combining handwork with a permanent record. But in practice, unskilled teachers use too much writing, and waste much of the precious time of the class period in trying to produce neat and complete notebooks.

"I have stopped using notebooks," a teacher told me recently. "We never have enough time. And there are so many other pleasant ways of self-expression and class activity." After spending a great deal of effort on notebooks, how many of you have come to about the same conclusion?

It is likely that the teacher who insists on perfect notebooks is only reflecting her own tidy personality, or trying to repeat some of the methods of her prim college days. She does not allow for the younger age of her pupils. Therefore, just to clear the air, let's ask ourselves, Why do we have pupil notebooks? Three main purposes come to mind, as follows:

(1) *Handwork, activity*—Observes one teacher, "At least my pupils are busy and quiet while they are writing." But surely this alone is a low motive. We have passed beyond mere "busy work." This motive might do for the substitute teacher, who must make the best use of the period. The trained teacher, with a larger vision of teaching, will scorn such an objective.

(2) *Self-expression, interpretation*—Here, as some one put it, "To know it, you must be able to say it. If you have to write it down, you fix the words in your mind." In theory, yes. But boys and girls from about the fourth grade through the eighth write very poorly and so slowly that the results are painful, or require much slow, patient supervision. And spelling is such a problem, especially with the many difficult Church words.

There are so many other ways of inducing expression. Many

children actually hate to write. The inarticulate child, asked to write out his sentence in silence, is apt to produce little of value. If the topic is thrown into the class for discussion, the best of all minds present is contributed. But when the conclusion is reached—usually phrased by the teacher—it can only be dictated, word for word, into all the notebooks. And the slowest pupil holds back the class. For this reason, notebooks of younger children usually end up about the same, with little originality developed.

(3) *Summary, for review*—High school and college pupils may thus use their notebooks, but is this of much value for juniors? There are so many other better ways. Do you still use the easily remembered catch-phrases to recall each lesson—Abraham, the friend of God, Joseph the dreamer, etc.? Such titles, with the dates taught, may well be written on a heavy cardboard (not the blackboard, which gets erased) from week to week, left hanging in the class room, and used frequently for drill. This takes no trouble, wastes no time. Moreover, frequent class drill is swifter, more thorough, than by the use of notebooks.

Here are some better uses of notebooks, if you still want them:

(1) *New words*—This is a section in the back of notebooks where any new word which arises in class is written, with a brief definition, and later used in sentences.

(2) *Things to look up*—The teacher says, "We haven't time to find out about that just now. Let's put it in our notebooks, and we'll see who will be the first to report on it." They turn to a section marked "Find out," and write down the item, as, "How many people can be seated in our church?" As they do this, previous questions inserted there are noticed, and perhaps the urge re-aroused to look them up, too.

(3) *Exchange books*—For this, books are exchanged around the class, and pupils mark for accuracy, neatness, originality.

Better than individual books is the Class Diary, kept by a student secretary—the office a high honor, and rotated frequently. The class starts with the reading of the record of the previous lesson, a much swifter way to review and get in motion than the usual, "Now, what did we talk about last Sunday?"

Into the Diary go all the points that arise in class—the summary of discussions, plans for the future, promises, assignments. One week the record reads, "We made plans for the basket. Joanne reported on the party. We talked about how to be helpful. We decided we must give people what they really need, not what we like." The smartest members of the class usually serve as secretary, and thereby a certain amount of special ability is directed and developed. Some touching and unexpected impressions may be recorded! A teacher found in looking over the Class Diary for the preceding Sunday, when she had been absent, and an old saint of the parish had been the substitute, the record was simply, "She talked to us about God."

The lure of well-kept notebooks undoubtedly has helped the vogue of the new workbooks, which seem to promise complete and tidy results with little effort. But those who have used them for a while will tell you how deceptive the results are. Notebooks, of any kind, are only a device, and must never become an end. The best that may be said for them is that they provide a chance for individual work and a feeling of personal possession and achievement. And they are at least a variation from the incessant talk of some teachers.

10. CLASSROOM DRAMATICS

Some time, after you have run through all the other ways of activity in class, you may decide to try "acting it out." It is much easier than it may seem at first thought. But it does take some advance thought, is never actually impromptu. Some teachers do it instinctively. But we would all do it now and then, if we would see the possibilities, and discover the fun of it.

Here is the way it works. A fifth grade class has just finished its planned work. The teacher has decided to use dramatics to develop the lesson further. Joseph is sold into Egypt (Genesis, chap. 37). It is full of possibilities, and there are plenty of characters. For instance:

Teacher (who has thought it out thoroughly, in advance): "If we should act this story out, who would be the main character? Where is the scene?" (Note: Don't call for a class decision too quickly, just as when launching a major project, but get their imagination rolling first. "*If* we acted. . . ." They will begin to respond in a few minutes, and then things will move, by a common mind and impulse.)

Teacher: "I'll ask Walter to pretend he is Joseph. Now Walter, what was the errand your father Jacob asked you to do?" (Walter replies.)

Teacher: "You might walk along here, Walter, no, *Joseph*, wondering where you would find your brothers and their sheep. As you go along, what are you thinking about? Have you had any dreams lately?"

Walter has his place now, and the others are in it too, making suggestions.

Teacher: "We'd better have the brothers over here. What are some of your names? What should the brothers be doing?" (Sitting around the camp.) "What are they talking about? Then, which one suddenly sees Joseph coming?"

So the story is recalled, and the setting and actions are sketched. Then the teacher says, "Now let's go through it again from the beginning."

Lines spoken, of course, are made up by the actors. No properties or costumes are needed. From sitting around a table, the group is suddenly acting. The teacher is stage-manager, drill-master, yet the pupils do much of the inventing. Thus:

Teacher: "How shall we have Joseph in the pit? Here—he can be just on the other side of this chair, on the floor."

There will be some horseplay and gaiety, yet it is surprising how seriously children take hold of such imaginative activity. If you don't believe it, try working out some past story you have studied. And remember, they like to repeat a successful enactment, especially if a new audience can be found, such as before the department opening, or at a parents' meeting. One excellent way is to have a neighboring class (by arrangement and permission) be the invited audience. In a pinch, this may be better than rushing in an unprepared substitute teacher.

A splendid example of Church School dramatics was given in the motion picture, "The Bells of St. Mary's," with Bing Crosby and Ingrid Bergman, where the primary children in the parochial school give their rendition of the Christmas story.

A small boy enters and announces, "We are going to tell you about the Baby Jesus. I am Joseph. This is Mary. We are going to Bethlehem." He assists Mary to a seat on the donkey (a sawhorse with a cardboard head, and a mop attached for tail, clearly the children's own creation).

"She is very tired. We have travelled a long way," says Joseph. There is a pause, then: "That's the end of the first scene." He then goes to an opening in the back curtain, saying, "Knock, knock."

A child sticks his head out, and there is a conversation about getting a room. It develops that Joseph has no money, so, no room. He reports this to Mary, still on the donkey, who accepts it cheerfully, saying, "Then why don't you try next door?" Here Joseph says, "And that's the end of that scene."

Joseph then tries an opening in the curtain farther along, and in a conversation with another speaker who sticks his head

through the curtain, finally arranges that Mary shall rest in the barn.

The donkey is dragged off by willing hands, and, after some delay, the curtains are pulled back to reveal the Nativity tableau. A cheerful baby about a year and a half old is in a laundry basket. (He refuses to lie down, but stands up all through the action, smiling at the audience.) An angel with paper wings stands on a stepladder. There are shepherds and a toy lamb, all introduced by brief sentences from Joseph.

"And here comes the neighbors, bringing some presents," as other children enter, placing objects before the crib (basket). "And now we will sing our Christmas song," Joseph announces, and leads them in the singing of "Happy birthday to you. Happy birthday, dear Jesus, happy birthday to you."

Several points in the foregoing might be noted which mark it as good teaching methods. Although only a scene from a movie, there is behind it much careful checking with a real school. Note the following:

(1) There were few properties or costumes, and even those were common objects at hand. The imagination provides practically everything. It is activity and self-expression on the most immediate level of spontaneous action.

(2) The teacher did not appear in the performance at all, not even in scene shifting or prompting. Everything was done by the children, in the final performance. They were not putting on a show, in the adult notion of a finished performance, but they were living through an experience, in their own terms.

(3) The lines were entirely made up by the children, and evidently changed every time they did it. The most ready speaker was given the major part. It was a favorite story, acted out whenever they could get an audience. Or, just for their own pleasure.

(4) The teacher clearly had put in her constructive sugges-

tions while the play was in process of being formulated, but had never intruded adult ideas. We are to imagine that the points were developed in several happy class periods in the weeks preceding. The idea of the donkey had fascinated them, and so they had created one, with head and tail complete. The reason for rejection at the inn was that the holy couple were poor, and hence the conversation about money. The thought of "Where can we find a Baby Jesus?" brought out the offer of somebody's baby brother. Angels being up in the air suggested the stepladder. And the "Happy Birthday" song seems far closer to childhood than even the customary "Silent Night."

All through, one can imagine much vital class discussion, a truly "socialized recitation" directed by the plan and oversight of the teacher, yet free enough to allow for every original idea that arose.

In the use of class room dramatics, four suggestions might be given:

(1) Have the scenes and action well thought out in the teacher's preparation, but present it *as if* spontaneous and worked out by the children. Such directed discussion will increase one's skill immensely in the use of the creative methods of project teaching. For the acting is a project, an outcome of the lesson, along the line of natural interests.

(2) Assign the characters yourself, at first. The reason is that the children make it a popularity contest, or else the most agressive demands a part. And all this wastes a lot of time. You can then change the parts around for a repeat, and they do love to reënact a favorite story.

(3) While directing the first action, be alert to accept every good suggestion offered, as to properties, lines, or business.

(4) Save this for the *end* of your period, as a relief from restlessness. Moreover, you can use up all your scant time with it, if you aren't careful.

Chancel pageantry is well recognized, and can be kept simple if sincerely done. There are enough properties at hand: a chair, a bench, a prayer desk, a small table, a screen. One child can announce the setting and subject. The question is often raised, Should we allow pupils to portray the person of our Lord? Why not? Doubtless this objection comes from adults who have witnessed various Passion Plays, where literalism and much sentimentality intrude, or the actor who took the part of Christ seemed inadequate. Others have a real feeling that no one is worthy to take the part. Yet with children, none of these objections obtain—certainly not with boys and girls up to fourteen. To avoid any seeming irreverence, the teacher must take pains to create the atmosphere of earnestness, and cause the assignment to be felt as a solemn privilege.

We might try class room dramatics more frequently. For example, there is the Easter story, rich in possibilities, yet (because of an overcrowded Lent) seldom stressed. We come upon Easter without warning, the stress of Holy Week takes up all the thought and energy of clergy and leaders, and the story of the Resurrection gets little more than a brief telling. But what a chance for the children! There are angels, and soldiers, the Marys, Peter and John, and the risen Lord. There can be added the upper room, and the Emmaus incident. There is plenty of dialog possible, easily invented or paraphrased. Ask your class how they would make it into a play, and immediately you will be astonished to see it taking shape from the children's suggestions. But before that, you must have *told* the story so well that it is recalled vividly.

Dramatization is a fine review, good physical activity, and gives scope for interpretation and imagination. It is loads of fun.

VII. A LAST WORD: THE REAL REASON

We started this book by proposing that you might consider Church School teaching as a hobby. We hoped to touch a certain inner corner of your mind, to catch you on one of your mild enthusiasms, on the rising up-swing of your best, responsive self. It was to be an appeal to a vague yearning, as yet unfocused on any special work, to be doing something for the sheer satisfaction of it. Some fuel was then provided for your imagination to play upon. By describing a variety of devices, and giving some hints, we tried to get you to see something of the inside of actual teaching, and that it is not beyond your ability.

In doing this, we followed the *educational method*—that is, we took you as (we imagined) we found you, and tried, with our best ingenuity, to get you warmed up and started. (We didn't want to discourage you, to lose you in the early stages.) Our problem was to *contact* you, as you were at the moment of starting this book. That is, we had to touch both your mind and your feelings and get them to vibrating to our proposition. ("Create interest, building on already existing interests" is the formula.)

"Aha! Teaching is just *salesmanship*," I hear somebody say. My child, don't let me ever hear you use that word again around the Church! It is a street word, used only by vulgar people driven solely by the profit motive. It is true that outwardly the salesman and the teacher *seem* to operate on the same lines. They approach their "prospect"* on the side of his known interests, enthusiasms, or desires and win his confidence. At the right stage both try to secure a decision. But the difference is in *why* each is operating. Salesmen too often are only interested in getting their commissions, and in nothing else. Teachers—certainly splendid Church School teachers—are motivated by the love of Christ. Their labors are completely unselfish, entirely sacrificial. "For *their* sakes. . . ."

This is where we came in. But there is something beyond all this, something closer to our heart's deepest desire. This is really a religious urge: we want to help children in their *religion*. At our best, we know that Bible stories and activities are not the real goals. We want to help them know God.

One time while I was calling at the home of a teacher, we were discussing how to make our pupils feel the personal reality of God. I said, "Do you think we teachers speak of God often enough in our lessons?"

A child of the family, who had been listening to our conversation, hung on the arm of my chair and said eagerly, "All right then, let's talk about God!"

It was perfectly natural and real. He was genuinely interested, curious in the most elemental way, and looked to adults for help. Notice that he did not ask any question about God. He wanted to *discuss* God, to enlarge his own notions by comparing them with those of others. He wanted no authoritative pronouncements, but a sharing of the thoughts he already had on the subject. This clear, native urge is something we miss so often in our heavy-handed approach to the teaching moment. We *tell* them about God, and since our own terms are often somewhat pedantic, we close the door of interest almost with our first words.

* The Church has, in recent years, borrowed this word from salesmanship, it is true, but with what a different intent!

Few adults can talk simply, sincerely, and winsomely about God. They have never tried, or they have felt self-conscious or argumentative. We assume that others "have their own religion" which we will not venture to intrude upon. But isn't it possible that we have never thought out clearly and completely the reality of God and His work in us? Our ideas are vague and unexpressed, and may be so until the end of our days.

They may be, that is, unless we find times when, with tender open souls—like children—we can honestly try to frame our blundering, groping notions and voice them in clear and straightforward conversation. For conversation and sharing it must be, not merely a grown-up phrasing of words. It must be testimony, witnessing, not second-hand reports. Nor must it be thin sentiment, or wordy piety. It must be talk that tries out words known and used by children, and which aims at sharing our larger spiritual experiences, if only for a brief moment, on their level.

This is the inward reward of being a teacher for God: that you learn by teaching. Teachers must know, *now*; other people may coast along the rest of their lives, knowing they can look it up if the need arises. So you master your subject matter— for their sakes.

But deeper than this familiar experience of the content, is the discovery of the *meaning* of the Faith: the personal relation of each soul with God Himself. You never really know until you have to submit your inner life to the requirements of a discussion period when, accidentally or planned, someone proposes, "Let's talk about God."

This is one of those rare *teaching moments* for which all the rest is only a preliminary. Here is the fine, front line of the advancing Faith of Christ, where souls meet souls and share.

Minds must meet. And since the subject of our talk will be

God Himself, we can be sure He is brooding over the moment, entering into the conversation. Here is the *occasion* for inspiration, rightly understood. The stage is set, or found; all is ready. Preparation is possible, but exact outlines fail us in conversation, especially with children. We cannot be sure what our pupils will say, and their emerging ideas must be met. Such moments are often short, and soon passed. But they are real, and we can learn to grasp them.

The presentation of the truths of the Christian religion to satisfy the requirements of individuals is known in academic circles as the art of apologetics. It is too often pursued as a theoretical contest, in the argument *ad hominem*, too often addressed to a *hominem* who died a generation ago, or is pure fiction. At its best, it means a skilful presentation of the Faith in a form acceptable to the actual person you are addressing, and in the context of the atmosphere in which you encounter him. You must take into consideration his age, his intelligence, his experiences, his prejudices. And the speaker is not to win a verbal victory, but to let God have His due.

What a long way this is from just telling Bible stories, and from all our patient drilling on facts! Here, if we will court them a little, and recognize them when they suddenly appear, may be times of deepest joy when, in our own character, we just talk about God. Can our Lord have been thinking of such moments of discipling when He promised, "It shall be given you in that hour what to speak"?